Speech-Grille

By Paul Celan:

Der Sand aus den Urnen
Mohn und Gedächtnis
Von Schwelle zu Schwelle
Sprachgitter
Die Niemandsrose
Atemwende
Fadensonnen
Lichtzwang

Translations by Joachim Neugroschel

RACINE: *Phaedra, Andromache*
CHEKHOV: *The Marriage Proposal*
BOSQUET: *Conversations with Dali*
MOLIÈRE: *Tartuffe, The Misanthrope*
JARRY: *Absolute Love*
ARP: *Arp on Arp*

Paul Celan
Speech-Grille

and Selected Poems

Translated by Joachim Neugroschel

E. P. Dutton & Co., Inc.
New York
1971

Acknowledgments

The translator wishes to thank the various people from whose advice and suggestions he feels he has profited in the course of doing these translations: Gusta Ewinger, Michael Roloff, and Ned Arnold.

English translation Copyright © 1971 by Joachim Neugroschel
Mohn und Gedächtnis © Deutsche Verlags-Anstalt GmbH, Stuttgart 1952;
Von Schwelle zu Schwelle © Deutsche Verlags-Anstalt GmbH, Stuttgart 1955;
Sprachgitter © S. Fischer Verlag Frankfurt am Main 1959; *Die Niemandsrose* © S. Fischer Verlag Frankfurt am Main 1963; *Atemwende* © Suhrkamp Verlag Frankfurt am Main 1967.

Published simultaneously in Canada by
Clarke, Irwin & Company, Limited, Toronto and Vancouver

Library of Congress Catalog Card Number: 78-133590
SBN: 0-525-20785-6 (cloth)   SBN: 0-525-04475-2 (paper)

Acknowledgment is hereby made to the following publications in which certain of these poems appeared in translation:

Harper's Magazine: "In the Shape of a Boar"; "Thread-suns"; "By All Means"; "Today and Tomorrow."

This book is dedicated
to Cheryl and to Warren

Contents

* Poems in italics are untitled.

6

Speech-Grille   Sprachgitter

7

from
The No-One's-Rose

aus
Die Niemandsrose

from
Breath-Turning

aus
Atemwende

8

9

aus
Mohn und Gedächtnis

from
Poppy and Memory

Marianne

Fliederlos ist dein Haar, dein Antlitz aus Spiegelglas.
Von Auge zu Aug zieht die Wolke, wie Sodom nach Babel:
wie Blattwerk zerpflückt sie den Turm und tobt um das Schwefel-
gesträuch.

Dann zuckt dir ein Blitz um den Mund—jene Schlucht mit den
Resten der Geige.
Mit schneeigen Zähnen führt einer den Bogen: O schöner tönte das
Schilf!

Geliebte, auch du bist das Schilf und wir alle der Regen;
ein Wein ohnegleichen dein Leib, und wir bechern zu zehnt;
ein Kahn im Getreide dein Herz, wir rudern ihn nachtwärts;
ein Krüglein Bläue, so hüpfest du leicht über uns, und wir
schlafen. . . .

Vorm Zelt zieht die Hundertschaft auf, und wir tragen dich
zechend zu Grabe.
Nun klingt auf den Fliesen der Welt der harte Taler der Träume.

Marianne

Your hair is lilac-less, your face is mirror-glass.
The cloud drifts from eye to eye, like Sodom to Babel:
it shreds the tower like leafage and rages around the sulphur-copse.

Then lightning flashes at your mouth—the gulf with the violin's
remnants.
Someone with snowy teeth wields the bow: oh finer the soughing of
sedge!

Beloved, you too are the sedge and the rest of us rain;
your body a peerless wine, and we topers are ten;
your heart a boat in the grain, we are rowing it nightwards;
a mug of blueness, lightly you hop over us, and we sleep. . . .

The hundred draw up at the tent, and swilling we bear you to the
grave.
Now the hard coin of dreams shocks on the flagging of the world.

Halbe Nacht

Halbe Nacht. Mit den Dolchen des Traumes geheftet in sprühende
Augen.
Schrei nicht vor Schmerz: wie Tücher flattern die Wolken.
Ein seidener Teppich, so ward sie gespannt zwischen uns, dass ge-
tanzt sei von Dunkel zu Dunkel.
Die schwarze Flöte schnitzten sie uns aus lebendigem Holz, und die
Tänzerin kommt nun.
Aus Meerschaum gesponnene Finger taucht sie ins Aug uns:
eines will hier noch weinen?
Keines. So wirbelt sie selig dahin, und die feurige Pauke wird laut.
Ringe wirft sie uns zu, wir fangen sie auf mit den Dolchen.
Vermählt sie uns so? Wie Scherben erklingts, und ich weiss es nun
wieder:
du starbst nicht
den malvenfarbenen Tod.

Half the Night

Half the night. Nailed by the daggers of dream to kindling eyes.
Don't scream in pain: the clouds are fluttering like cloth.
A silken carpet, the night was stretched between us, for dancing
                                     from darkness to darkness.
They carved the black flute for us of living wood, and now the
                                     dancer is coming.
She dips fingers spun of seafroth into our eye:
does any eye still wish to weep?
None. So she blissfully whirls away, and the fiery drum grows loud.
She throws rings at us, we catch them with the daggers.
Is she wedding us? The sound is like shards, and I realize again:
you did not die
the mauve death.

Der Sand aus den Urnen

Schimmelgrün ist das Haus des Vergessens.
Vor jedem der wehenden Tore blaut dein enthaupteter Spielmann.
Er schlägt dir die Trommel aus Moos und bitterem Schamhaar;
mit schwärender Zehe malt er im Sand deine Braue.
Länger zeichnet er sie als sie war, und das Rot deiner Lippe.
Du füllst hier die Urnen und speisest dein Herz.

The Sand from the Urns

Moldy-green is the house of oblivion.
At each of the wavering gates your beheaded minstrel turns blue.
He beats the drum for you of moss and bitter pubic hair;
with a festering toe he paints your eyebrow in sand.
He draws it longer than it was, and the red of your lip.
You fill the urns here and nourish your heart.

Das Gastmahl

Geleert sei die Nacht aus den Flaschen im hohen Gebälk der Versu-
chung,
die Schwelle mit Zähnen gepflügt, vor Morgen der Jähzorn gesät:
es schiesst wohl empor uns ein Moos noch, eh von der Mühle sie hier
sind,
ein leises Getreide zu finden bei uns ihrem langsamen Rad . . .

Unter den giftigen Himmeln sind andere Halme wohl falber,
wird anders der Traum noch gemünzt als hier, wo wir würfeln um
Lust,
als hier, wo getauscht wird im Dunkel Vergessen und Wunder,
wo alles nur gilt eine Stunde und schwelgend bespien wird von uns,
ins gierige Wasser der Fenster geschleudert in leuchtenden
Truhen—:
es birst auf der Strasse der Menschen, den Wolken zum Ruhm!

So hüllet euch denn in die Mäntel und steiget mit mir auf die
Tische:
wie anders sei noch geschlafen als stehend, inmitten der Kelche?
Wem trinken wir Träume noch zu, als dem langsamen Rad?

The Banquet

Let the night be drained from the flasks in the lofty rafters of tempt-
ing,
the threshold be plowed with teeth, the choler sown before morn-
ing:
a moss will doubtless spring up for us before they arrive from the
mill
to find a quiet grain with us their gradual wheel. . . .

Under the venomous heavens other stalks are probably paler
a dream is otherwise minted than here where we dice for pleasure,
than here where oblivion and miracle are traded in darkness
where anything counts but an hour and is spit at in our carousing,
and hurled in luminous chests into greedy water of windows—:
it bursts on the highway of humans for the glory of clouds!

Then wrap yourselves up in the cloaks and climb with me on the
tables:
how else shall we sleep but erect, amidst the cups?
To whom shall we drink and pledge dreams but the gradual wheel?

Dunkles Aug im September

Steinhaube Zeit. Und üppiger quellen
die Locken des Schmerzes ums Antlitz der Erde,
den trunkenen Apfel, gebräunt von dem Hauch
eines sündigen Spruches: schön und abhold dem Spiel,
das sie treiben im argen
Widerschein ihrer Zukunft.

Zum zweitenmal blüht die Kastanie:
ein Zeichen der ärmlich entbrannten
Hoffnung auf Orions
baldige Rückkunft: der blinden
Freunde des Himmels sternklare Inbrunst
ruft ihn herauf.

Unverhüllt an den Toren des Traumes
streitet ein einsames Aug.
Was täglich geschieht,
genügt ihm zu wissen:
am östlichen Fenster
erscheint ihm zur Nachtzeit die schmale
Wandergestalt des Gefühls.

Ins Nass ihres Auges tauchst du das Schwert.

Dark Eye in September

Stone-hood: Time. And lusher, the curls
of pain swell over the face of the earth,
the drunken apple, burnished by the breath
of a sinful decree: fine and averse to the game
which they play in the vile
reflection of their future.

The chestnut blossoms a second time:
a sign of the poorly enkindled
hope for Orion's
speedy return: the star-clear
ardor of heaven's blind friends
summons him up.

Exposed at the doorway to dreams
a lonesome eye is fighting.
What happens each day
is all it need know:
at the eastern window
the slender wanderer-phantom
of feeling appears at night.

In the wet of its eye you dip the sword.

Lob der Ferne

Im Quell deiner Augen
leben die Garne der Fischer der Irrsee.
Im Quell deiner Augen
hält das Meer sein Versprechen.

Hier werf ich,
ein Herz, das geweilt unter Menschen,
die Kleider von mir und den Glanz eines Schwures:

Schwärzer im Schwarz, bin ich nackter.
Abtrünnig erst bin ich treu.
Ich bin du, wenn ich ich bin.

Im Quell deiner Augen
treib ich und träume von Raub.

Ein Garn fing ein Garn ein:
wir scheiden umschlungen.

Im Quell deiner Augen
erwürgt ein Gehenkter den Strang.

In Praise of Remoteness

In the wellspring of your eyes
live the fish-nets of the labyrinth-sea.
In the wellspring of your eyes
the ocean keeps its promise.

Here I,
a heart that lingered among men,
cast off my clothes and the luster of a vow:

Blacker in black, I am nuder.
Only when faithless am I true.
I am you when I am I.

In the wellspring of your eyes
I drift and I dream about prey.

A net snared a net:
we separate entwined.

In the wellspring of your eyes
a hanged man strangles the rope.

Spät und Tief

Boshaft wie goldene Rede beginnt diese Nacht.
Wir essen die Äpfel der Stummen.
Wir tuen ein Werk, das man gern seinem Stern überlässt;
wir stehen im Herbst unsrer Linden als sinnendes Fahnenrot,
als brennende Gäste vom Süden.
Wir schwören bei Christus dem Neuen, den Staub zu vermählen
dem Staube,
die Vögel dem wandernden Schuh,
unser Herz einer Stiege im Wasser.
Wir schwören der Welt die heiligen Schwüre des Sandes,
wir schwören sie gern,
wir schwören sie laut von den Dächern des traumlosen Schlafes
und schwenken das Weisshaar der Zeit . . .

Sie rufen: Ihr lästert!

Wir wissen es längst.
Wir wissen es längst, doch was tuts?
Ihr mahlt in den Mühlen des Todes das weisse Mehl der Verheis-
sung,
ihr setzet es vor unsern Brüdern und Schwestern—

Wir schwenken das Weisshaar der Zeit.

Ihr mahnt uns: Ihr lästert!
Wir wissen es wohl,
es komme die Schuld über uns.
Es komme die Schuld über uns aller warnenden Zeichen,
es komme das gurgelnde Meer,
der geharnischte Windstoss der Umkehr,
der mitternächtige Tag,
es komme, was niemals noch war!

Es komme ein Mensch aus dem Grabe.

Late and Deep

Spiteful as golden speech this night begins.
We are eating the apples of mutes.
We are doing a work that one gladly leaves to one's star;
we stand in the fall of our lindens as wistful vexillum-red,
as ardent guests from the south.
We swear by Christ the New One to marry the dust to the dust,
the birds to the wandering shoe,
our heart to a stairway in water,
We swear to the world the sacred vows of the sand,
we swear them gladly,
we swear them aloud from the rooftops of dreamless sleep
and whisk the white-hair of time . . .

They shout: You blaspheme!

We have known it long since.
We have known it long since, but what of it?
In the mills of death you grind the white meal of Promise,
you set it before our brothers and sisters—

We whisk the white-hair of time.

You warn us: You blaspheme!
We know we do,
let the guilt come upon us.
Let the guilt come upon us of all warning signs,
let the gurgling ocean come,
the emphatic gust of reversal,
the midnight day,
let come what never was!

Let a man come forth from the tomb.

Corona

Aus der Hand frisst der Herbst mir sein Blatt: wir sind Freunde.
Wir schälen die Zeit aus den Nüssen und lehren sie gehn:
die Zeit kehrt zurück in die Schale.

Im Spiegel ist Sonntag,
im Traum wird geschlafen,
der Mund redet wahr.

Mein Aug steigt hinab zum Geschlecht der Geliebten:
wir sehen uns an,
wir sagen uns Dunkles,
wir lieben einander wie Mohn und Gedächtnis,
wir schlafen wie Wein in den Muscheln,
wie das Meer im Blutstrahl des Mondes.

Wir stehen umschlungen im Fenster, sie sehen uns zu von der
Strasse:
es ist Zeit, dass man weiss!
Es ist Zeit, dass der Stein sich zu blühen bequemt,
dass der Unrast ein Herz schlägt.
Es ist Zeit, dass es Zeit wird.

Es ist Zeit.

Corona

The fall eats its leaf from my hand: we are friends.
We now shuck time from the nuts and teach it to walk:
time returns to the shell.

In the mirror it's Sunday,
in the dream there is sleeping,
the mouth speaks truth.

My eye descends to the sex of the beloved:
we gaze at one another,
we speak dark things,
we love one another like poppy and memory,
we sleep like wine in the conches,
like the sea in the blood-beam of moon.

We stand entwined at the window, they look at us from the street:
it is time people knew!
It is time that the stone condescended to bloom,
that a heart beat for unrest.
It is time it were time.

It is time.

Todesfuge

Schwarze Milch der Frühe wir trinken sie abends
wir trinken sie mittags und morgens wir trinken sie nachts
wir trinken und trinken
wir schaufeln ein Grab in den Lüften da liegt man nicht eng
Ein Mann wohnt im Haus der spielt mit den Schlangen der schreibt
der schreibt wenn es dunkelt nach Deutschland dein goldenes Haar
Margarete
er schreibt es und tritt vor das Haus und es blitzen die Sterne er
pfeift seine Rüden herbei
er pfeift seine Juden hervor lässt schaufeln ein Grab in der Erde
er befiehlt uns spielt auf nun zum Tanz

Schwarze Milch der Frühe wir trinken dich nachts
wir trinken dich morgens und mittags wir trinken dich abends
wir trinken und trinken
Ein Mann wohnt im Haus und spielt mit den Schlangen der schreibt
der schreibt wenn es dunkelt nach Deutschland dein goldenes Haar
Margarete
Dein aschenes Haar Sulamith wir schaufeln ein Grab in den Lüften
da liegt man nicht eng

Er ruft stecht tiefer ins Erdreich ihr einen ihr andern singet und
spielt
er greift nach dem Eisen im Gurt er schwingts seine Augen sind
blau
stecht tiefer die Spaten ihr einen ihr andern spielt weiter zum Tanz
auf

Schwarze Milch der Frühe wir trinken dich nachts
wir trinken dich mittags und morgens wir trinken dich abends

Death Fugue

Black milk of dawn we drink it at dusk
we drink it at noon and at daybreak we drink it at night
we drink and we drink
we are digging a grave in the air there's room for us all
A man lives in the house he plays with the serpents he writes
he writes when it darkens to Germany your golden hair Margarete
he writes it and steps outside and the stars all aglisten he whistles for
                                         his hounds
he whistles for his Jews he has them dig a grave in the earth
he commands us to play for the dance

Black milk of dawn we drink you at night
we drink you at daybreak and noon we drink you at dusk
we drink and we drink
A man lives in the house he plays with the serpents he writes
he writes when it darkens to Germany your golden hair Margarete
Your ashen hair Shulamite we are digging a grave in the air there's
                                         room for us all

He shouts cut deeper in the earth to some the rest of you sing and
                                         play
he reaches for the iron in his belt he heaves it his eyes are blue
make your spades cut deeper the rest of you play for the dance

Black milk of dawn we drink you at night
we drink you at noon and at daybreak we drink you at dusk

wir trinken und trinken
ein Mann wohnt im Haus dein goldenes Haar Margarete
dein aschenes Haar Sulamith er spielt mit den Schlangen

Er ruft spielt süsser den Tod der Tod ist ein Meister aus Deutsch-
land
er ruft streicht dunkler die Geigen dann steigt ihr als Rauch in die
Luft
dann habt ihr ein Grab in den Wolken da liegt man nicht eng

Schwarze Milch der Frühe wir trinken dich nachts
wir trinken dich mittags der Tod ist ein Meister aus Deutschland
wir trinken dich abends und morgens wir trinken und trinken
der Tod ist ein Meister aus Deutschland sein Auge ist blau
er trifft dich mit bleierner Kugel er trifft dich genau
ein Mann wohnt im Haus dein goldenes Haar Margarete
er hetzt seine Rüden auf uns er schenkt uns ein Grab in der Luft
er spielt mit den Schlangen und träumet der Tod ist ein Meister aus
Deutschland

dein goldenes Haar Margarete
dein aschenes Haar Sulamith

we drink and we drink
a man lives in the house your golden hair Margarete
your ashen hair Shulamite he plays with the serpents

He shouts play death more sweetly death is a master from Germany
he shouts play the violins darker you'll rise as smoke in the air
then you'll have a grave in the clouds there's room for you all

Black milk of dawn we drink you at night
we drink you at noon death is a master from Germany
we drink you at dusk and at daybreak we drink and we drink you
death is a master from Germany his eye is blue
he shoots you with bullets of lead his aim is true
a man lives in the house your golden hair Margarete
he sets his hounds on us he gives us a grave in the air
he plays with the serpents and dreams death is a master from
                                                          Germany

your golden hair Margarete
your ashen hair Shulamite

In Ägypten

Du sollst zum Aug der Fremden sagen: Sei das Wasser.
Du sollst, die du im Wasser seisst, im Aug der Fremden suchen.
Du sollst sie rufen aus dem Wasser: Ruth! Noëmi! Mirjam!
Du sollst sie schmücken, wenn du bei der Fremden liegst.
Du sollst sie schmücken mit dem Wolkenhaar der Fremden.
Du sollst zu Ruth und Mirjam und Noëmi sagen:
Seht, ich schlaf bei ihr!
Du sollst die Fremde neben dir am schönsten schmücken.
Du sollst sie schmücken mit dem Schmerz um Ruth, um Mirjam
                                                    und Noëmi.
Du sollst zur Fremden sagen:
Sieh, ich schlief bei diesen!

In Egypt

Thou shalt say to the eye of the strange woman: Be the water.
Thou shalt seek in the eye of the strange woman those whom you
know to be in the water.
Thou shalt call them forth from the water: Ruth! Naomi! Miriam!
Thou shalt adorn them when you lie with the strange woman.
Thou shalt adorn them with the cloud-hair of the strange woman.
Thou shalt say to Ruth and Miriam and Naomi:
Behold, I sleep with her!
Thou shalt adorn most beautifully the strange woman next to you.
Thou shalt adorn her with the grief for Ruth, for Miriam and
Naomi.
Thou shalt say to the strange woman:
Behold, I slept with them!

Wer wie du und alle Tauben Tag und Abend aus dem Dunkel
                                                    schöpft,

pickt den Stern aus meinen Augen, eh er funkelt,
reisst das Gras aus meinen Brauen, eh es weiss ist,
wirft die Tür zu in den Wolken, eh ich stürze.

Wer wie du und alle Nelken Blut als Münze braucht und Tod als
                                                    Wein,

bläst das Glas für seinen Kelch aus meinen Händen,
färbt es mit dem Wort, das ich nicht sagte, rot,
schlägts in Stücke mit dem Stein der fernen Träne.

Whoever like you and all doves drains day and evening from dark-
ness,

he pecks the star from my eye before it glitters,
rips the grass from my brows before it turns white,
slams the door in the clouds before I hurtle.

Whoever like you and all carnations uses blood as coin and death as
wine,

he blows the glass for his goblet from my hands,
stains it red with the word I did not speak,
shatters it with the stone of the faraway tear.

Brandmal

Wir schliefen nicht mehr, denn wir lagen im Uhrwerk der Schwer-
mut

und bogen die Zeiger wie Ruten,
und sie schnellten zurück und peitschten die Zeit bis aufs Blut,
und du redetest wachsenden Dämmer,
und zwölfmal sagte ich du zur Nacht deiner Worte,
und sie tat sich auf und blieb offen,
und ich legt ihr ein Aug in den Schoss und flocht dir das andre ins
Haar

und schlang zwischen beide die Zündschnur, die offene Ader—
und ein junger Blitz schwamm heran.

Stigma

We slept no more for we lay in the clockwork of sorrow
and bent the hands like rods,
and they bolted back and scourged time till blood was drawn,
and you spoke a gathering twilight,
and twelve times I said thou to the night of your words,
and it opened and stayed apart,
and I put one eye in its lap and plaited one in your hair
and I twisted the fuse between them, the open vein—
and a young flash of lightning came floating.

Kristall

Nicht an meinen Lippen suche deinen Mund
nicht vorm Tor den Fremdling,
nicht im Aug die Träne.

Sieben Nächte höher wandert Rot zu Rot,
sieben Herzen tiefer pocht die Hand ans Tor,
sieben Rosen später rauscht der Brunnen.

Crystal

Do not seek your mouth at my lips
nor the stranger before the gate,
nor the tear in the eye.

Seven nights higher, red wanders to red,
seven hearts deeper, the hand knocks at the gate,
seven roses later, the well moans.

Die Krüge

Für Klaus Demus

An den langen Tischen der Zeit
zechen die Krüge Gottes.
Sie trinken die Augen der Sehenden leer und die Augen der
                                                    Blinden,
die Herzen der waltenden Schatten,
die hohle Wange des Abends.
Sie sind die gewaltigsten Zecher:
sie führen das Leere zum Mund wie das Volle
und schäumen nicht über wie du oder ich.

The Tankards

for Klaus Demus

At the long tables of time
the tankards of God are carousing.
They drain the eyes of the seeing and the eyes of the blind,
the hearts of the governing shadows,
the hollow cheek of the evening.
They are the mightiest carousers:
they raise both the empty and full to their lips
and never foam over as you do or I.

Schlaf und Speise

Der Hauch der Nacht ist dein Laken, die Finsternis legt sich zu dir.
Sie rührt dir an Knöchel und Schläfe, sie weckt dich zu Leben und
Schlaf,
sie spürt dich im Wort auf, im Wunsch, im Gedanken,
sie schläft bei jedem von ihnen, sie lockt dich hervor.
Sie kämmt dir das Salz aus den Wimpern und tischt es dir auf,
sie lauscht deinen Stunden den Sand ab und setzt ihn dir vor.
Und was sie als Rose war, Schatten und Wasser,
schenkt sie dir ein.

Food and Slumber

The breath of night is your sheet, the darkness lies down with you.
It nudges your ankle and temple, it wakes you to life and to sleep,
it stalks you down in words, in wishes, in thoughts,
it sleeps with each one of them, it lures you forth.
It combs the salt from your lashes and serves it to you,
it learns the sand from your hours and sets it before you.
And what it was as a rose, shadow and water,
it pours in your cup.

Zähle die Mandeln

Zähle die Mandeln,
zähle, was bitter war und dich wachhielt,
zähl mich dazu:

Ich suchte dein Aug, als du's aufschlugst und niemand dich ansah,
ich spann jenen heimlichen Faden,
an dem der Tau, den du dachtest,
hinunterglitt zu den Krügen,
die ein Spruch, der zu niemandes Herz fand, behütet.

Dort erst tratest du ganz in den Namen, der dein ist,
schrittest du sicheren Fusses zu dir,
schwangen die Hämmer frei im Glockenstuhl deines Schweigens,
stiess das Erlauschte zu dir,
legte das Tote den Arm auch um dich,
und ihr ginget selbdritt durch den Abend.

Mache mich bitter.
Zähle mich zu den Mandeln.

Count the Almonds

Count the almonds,
count what was bitter and kept you awake,
count me along:

I looked for your eye when you raised it and nobody watched you,
I spun that secret thread
on which the dew, that you thought,
slipped down to the jugs
all guarded by a decree that found nobody's heart.

It was there that you first entered fully the name which is yours,
that you strode to yourself with sure feet
that the hammers heaved free in the bell-yoke of your silence,
that the hearkened joined you,
that the dead put its arm around you too,
and the three of you walked through the evening.

Make me bitter.
Count me along with the almonds.

aus
Von Schwelle zu Schwelle

from
Threshold to Threshold

Zwiegestalt

Lass dein Aug in der Kammer sein eine Kerze,
den Blick einen Docht,
lass mich blind genug sein,
ihn zu entzünden.

Nein.
Lass anderes sein.

Tritt vor dein Haus,
schirr deinen scheckigen Traum an,
lass seine Hufe reden
zum Schnee, den du fortbliest
vom First meiner Seele.

Double-Shape

Let your eye be a candle in the chamber,
your gaze a wick,
let me be blind enough
to ignite it.

No.
Let it be otherwise.

Step from your house,
harness your dappled dream,
let its hooves speak
to the snow you blew
off the ridge of my soul.

Fernen

Aug in Aug, in der Kühle,
lass uns auch solches beginnen:
gemeinsam
lass uns atmen den Schleier,
der uns voreinander verbirgt,
wenn der Abend sich anschickt zu messen,
wie weit es noch ist
von jeder Gestalt, die er annimmt,
zu jeder Gestalt,
die er uns beiden geliehn.

Distances

Eye in eye, in the coolness,
let us begin such things too:
together
let us breathe the veil
that hides us from one another
when the evening makes ready to measure
how far it still is
from every shape it assumes
to every shape
it bestows on us both.

In Gestalt eines Ebers

In Gestalt eines Ebers
stampft dein Traum durch die Wälder am Rande des Abends.
Blitzendweiss
wie das Eis, aus dem er hervorbrach,
sind seine Hauer.

Eine bittere Nuss
wühlt er hervor unterm Laub,
das sein Schatten den Bäumen entriss,
eine Nuss,
schwarz wie das Herz, das dein Fuss vor sich herstiess,
als du selber hier schrittst.

Er spiesst sie auf
und erfüllt das Gehölz mit grunzendem Schicksal,
dann treibts ihn
hinunter zur Küste,
dorthin, wo das Meer
seiner Feste finsterstes gibt
auf den Klippen:

vielleicht
dass eine Frucht wie die seine
das feiernde Auge entzückt,
das solche Steine geweint hat.

In the Shape of a Boar

In the shape of a boar
your dream tramples through the woods on the edges of evening.
Glittering white
like the ice from which it erupted
are its razors.

It rakes up a bitter nut
from under the leaves
that its shadow tore from the trees,
a nut
black as the heart that your foot kicked along
when you walked here yourself.

It gores the nut
and fills the thicket with grunting fate,
then strikes off
down towards the coast,
there where the sea
holds its darkest of feasts
on the crags:

perhaps
a fruit like its own
will delight the festive eye
that has wept such stones.

Grabschrift für François

Die beiden Türen der Welt
stehen offen:
geöffnet von dir
in der Zwienacht.
Wir hören sie schlagen und schlagen
und tragen das ungewisse,
und tragen das Grün in dein Immer.

Oktober 1953

Epitaph for François

The two doors of the world
stand apart:
opened by you
in the twinight
We hear them banging and banging
and bearing the uncertain,
and bearing the Green in your Always.

October 1953

Aufs Auge gepfropft

Aufs Auge gepfropft
ist dir das Reis, das den Wäldern den Weg wies:
verschwistert den Blicken,
treibt es die schwarze,
die Knospe.

Himmelweit spannt sich das Lid diesem Frühling.
Lidweit dehnt sich der Himmel,
darunter, beschirmt von der Knospe,
der Ewige pflügt,
der Herr.

Lausche der Pflugschar, lausche.
Lausche: sie knirscht
über der harten, der hellen,
der unvordenklichen Träne.

Grafted on Your Eye

The twig that showed the woods their way
is grafted on your eye:
a sibling to the gazes
it sprouts the black,
the bud.

As wide as heaven the lid spans toward this springtime.
As wide as a lid, heaven stretches;
below, shielded by the bud,
the Eternal One plows,
the Lord.

Listen to the plowshare, listen.
Listen: it's crunching
over the hard, the bright,
the immemorial tear.

Vor einer Kerze

Aus getriebenem Golde, so
wie du's mir anbefahlst, Mutter,
formt ich den Leuchter, daraus
sie empor mir dunkelt inmitten
splitternder Stunden:
deines
Totseins Tochter.

Schlank von Gestalt,
ein schmaler, mandeläugiger Schatten,
Mund und Geschlecht
umtanzt von Schlummergetier,
entschwebt sie dem klaffenden Golde,
steigt sie hinan
zum Scheitel des Jetzt.

Mit nachtverhangnen
Lippen
sprech ich den Segen:

    Im Namen der Drei,
    die einander befehden, bis
    der Himmel hinabtaucht ins Grab der Gefühle,
    im Namen der Drei, deren Ringe
    am Finger mir glänzen, sooft
    ich den Bäumen im Abgrund das Haar lös,
    auf dass die Tiefe durchrauscht sei von reicherer Flut—,
    im Namen des ersten der Drei,
    der aufschrie,
    als es zu leben galt dort, wo vor ihm sein Wort schon gewesen,

Before a Candle

In hammered gold, just
as you directed, mother,
I formed the candlestick from which
she darkens upward to me amid
splintering hours:
your
death's daughter.

Of slender shape,
a slim, almond-eyed shadow,
her mouth and sex
rounded by dancing slumber-creatures,
she glides from the gaping gold,
she mounts
to the acme of now.

With night-hung
lips
I speak the blessing:

> In the name of the three
> who war with each other until
> the sky submerges in the grave of feelings,
> in the name of the three whose rings
> shine on my fingers whenever
> I loosen the hair of the trees in the gulf,
> so that a richer flood may roar through the depth—
> in the name of the first of the three,
> who screamed
> when he had to live where his word had already been,

im Namen des zweiten, der zusah und weinte,
im Namen des dritten, der weisse
Steine häuft in der Mitte,—
sprech ich dich frei
vom Amen, das uns übertäubt,
vom eisigen Licht, das es säumt,
da, wo es turmhoch ins Meer tritt,
da, wo die graue, die Taube
aufpickt die Namen
diesseits und jenseits des Sterbens:
Du bleibst, du bleibst, du bleibst
einer Toten Kind,
geweiht dem Nein meiner Sehnsucht,
vermählt einer Schrunde der Zeit,
vor die mich das Mutterwort führte,
auf dass ein einziges Mal
erzittre die Hand,
die je und je mir ans Herz greift!

in the name of the second, who witnessed and wept,
in the name of the third, who heaps
white stones in the middle—
I absolve you
of the amen that clamors us down,
of the icy light that edges it,
there where, towering, it enters the ocean,
there where the gray one, the dove,
pecks up the names
on either side of dying:
You remain, you remain, you remain
a dead woman's child,
hallowed to the No of my longing,
wedded to a fissure in time,
to which the maternal word brought me,
so that just once
the hand might shake
that never stops clutching the heart!

Die Halde

Neben mir lebst du, gleich mir:
als ein Stein
in der eingesunkenen Wange der Nacht.

O diese Halde, Geliebte,
wo wir pausenlos rollen,
wir Steine,
von Rinnsal zu Rinnsal.
Runder von Mal zu Mal.
Ähnlicher. Fremder.

O dieses trunkene Aug,
das hier umherirrt wie wir
und uns zuweilen
staunend in eins schaut.

The Scarp

You live next to me, like me:
as a stone
in the sunken cheek of the night.

Oh this scarp, beloved,
where we roll without rest,
we stones,
from rill to rill.
Rounder each time to each time.
More alike. More alien.

Oh this drunken eye
that roams around here as we do
and at times
amazed looks us into one.

Flügelnacht

Flügelnacht, weither gekommen und nun
für immer gespannt
über Kreide und Kalk.
Kiesel, abgrundhin rollend.
Schnee. Und mehr noch des Weissen.

Unsichtbar,
was braun schien,
gedankenfarben und wild
überwuchert von Worten.

Kalk ist und Kreide.
Und Kiesel.
Schnee. Und mehr noch des Weissen.

Du, du selbst:
in das fremde
Auge gebettet, das dies
überblickt.

Wing-Night

Wing-night, come from afar and now
spanned for ever
over chalk and lime.
Gravel, rolling gulfwards.
Snow. And still more of the white.

Invisible
what seemed brown,
thought-colored and rankly
overrun with words.

Lime, yes, and chalk.
And gravel.
Snow. And still more of the white.

You, yourself:
sheltered in the
alien eye that oversees
all this.

Welchen der Steine du hebst

Welchen der Steine du hebst—
du entblösst,
die des Schutzes der Steine bedürfen:
nackt,
erneuern sie nun die Verflechtung.

Welchen der Bäume du fällst—
du zimmerst
die Bettstatt, darauf
die Seelen sich abermals stauen,
als schütterte nicht
auch dieser
Äon.

Welches der Worte du sprichst—
du dankst
dem Verderben.

Whichever Stone You Lift

Whichever stone you lift—
you lay bare
those who need the protection of stones:
naked,
they now renew the intervolving.

Whichever tree you fell—
you construct
the bedstead on which
the souls jam up anew,
as if this eon
too did not
shake.

Whichever word you speak—
you thank
perdition.

Schibboleth

Mitsamt meinen Steinen,
den grossgeweinten
hinter den Gittern,

schleiften sie mich
in die Mitte des Marktes,
dorthin,
wo die Fahne sich aufrollt, der ich
keinerlei Eid schwor.

Flöte,
Doppelflöte der Nacht:
denke der dunklen
Zwillingsröte
in Wien und Madrid.

Setz deine Fahne auf Halbmast,
Erinnrung.
Auf Halbmast
für heute und immer.

Herz:
gib dich auch hier zu erkennen,
hier, in der Mitte des Marktes.
Ruf's, das Schibboleth, hinaus
in die Fremde der Heimat:
Februar. No pasarán.

Einhorn:
du weisst um die Steine,

Shibboleth

Along with my stones,
the hugely wept ones
behind the bars,

they dragged me to
the midst of the market,
there
where the flag unfurls to which
I swore no allegiance.

Flute,
double-flute of night:
think of the dark
twin-red
in Vienna and Madrid.

Fly your flag at halfmast,
memory.
At halfmast
today and forever.

Heart:
make yourself known even here,
here in the midst of the market.
Call it out, the shibboleth,
into the alien homeland:
February. No pasarán.

Unicorn:
you know about the stones,

du weisst um die Wasser,
komm,
ich führ dich hinweg
zu den Stimmen
von Estremadura.

you know about the waters,
come,
I will lead you across
to the voices
of Estremadura.

Die Winzer

Für Nani und Klaus Demus

Sie herbsten den Wein ihrer Augen,
sie keltern alles Geweinte, auch dieses:
so will es die Nacht,
die Nacht, an die sie gelehnt sind, die Mauer,
so forderts der Stein,
der Stein, über den ihr Krückstock dahinspricht
ins Schweigen der Antwort—
ihr Krückstock, der einmal,
einmal im Herbst,
wenn das Jahr zum Tod schwillt, als Traube,
der einmal durchs Stumme hindurchspricht, hinab
in den Schacht des Erdachten.

Sie herbsten, sie keltern den Wein,
sie pressen die Zeit wie ihr Auge,
sie kellern das Sickernde ein, das Geweinte,
im Sonnengrab, das sie rüsten
mit nachtstarker Hand:
auf dass ein Mund danach dürste, später—
ein Spätmund, ähnlich dem ihren:
Blindem entgegengekrümmt und gelähmt—
ein Mund, zu dem der Trunk aus der Tiefe emporschäumt, indes
der Himmel hinabsteigt ins wächserne Meer,
um fernher als Lichtstumpf zu leuchten,
wenn endlich die Lippe sich feuchtet.

The Vintagers

For Nani and Klaus Demus

They gather the grapes of their eyes,
they tread all weeping, even this:
the night wills it,
the night on which they are leaning, the wall,
the stone demands it,
the stone over which their cane speaks away
into the hush of the answer—
their cane that once,
once in autumn,
when the year swells towards death, as a cluster of grapes,
the cane that speaks once through the muteness, down
into the shaft of the imagined.

They gather, they tread the grapes,
they press time like their eye,
they cellar the seeping, the weeping,
in the sun's grave that they prepare
with a night-strong hand:
so that a mouth may thirst for it, later—
a late-mouth, akin to theirs:
bent towards blindness and paralyzed,
a mouth to which the draught foams up from the depth, while
the sky descends into the waxen sea
to glow from afar as a candle-stub
when the lip moistens at last.

Sprachgitter

Speech-Grille

Stimmen, ins Grün
der Wasserfläche geritzt.
Wenn der Eisvogel taucht,
sirrt die Sekunde:

Was zu dir stand
an jedem der Ufer,
es tritt
gemäht in ein anderes Bild.

*

Stimmen vom Nesselweg her:

Komm auf den Händen zu uns.
Wer mit der Lampe allein ist,
hat nur die Hand, draus zu lesen.

*

Stimmen, nachtdurchwachsen, Stränge,
an die du die Glocke hängst.

Wölbe dich, Welt:
Wenn die Totenmuschel heranschwimmt,
will es hier läuten.

*

Stimmen, vor denen dein Herz
ins Herz deiner Mutter zurückweicht.

Voices, nicked in
the green of the watery reach.
When the kingfisher dives
the moment buzzes:

What took your part
on each of the banks
it steps
mowed into another image.

*

Voices from the road of nettles:

Come on your hands to us.
Anyone alone with the lamp
has only his palm to read from.

*

Voices, marbled with night, ropes
on which you hang the bell.

Vault over, world:
when the seashell of death washes up
there will be a knelling.

*

Voices, from which your heart
shrinks back into your mother's heart.

Stimmen vom Galgenbaum her,
wo Spätholz und Frühholz die Ringe
tauschen und tauschen.

*

Stimmen, kehlig, im Grus,
darin auch Unendliches schaufelt,
(herz-)
schleimiges Rinnsal.

Setz hier die Boote aus, Kind,
die ich bemannte:

Wenn mittschiffs die Bö sich ins Recht setzt,
treten die Klammern zusammen.

*

Jakobsstimme:

Die Tränen.
Die Tränen im Bruderaug.
Eine blieb hängen, wuchs.
Wir wohnen darin.
Atme, dass
sie sich löse.

*

Stimmen im Innern der Arche:

Es sind
nur die Münder
geborgen. Ihr

Voices from the gallows-tree,
in which late wood and early wood
trade and trade the rings.

*

Voices, guttural, in the rubble
where endlessness also shovels,
(heart-)
mucous rill.

Child, here launch the boats
which I manned.

When amidships the squall takes control,
the clamps come together.

*

Jacob's voice:

The tears.
The tears in the brother's eye.
One clung, grew.
We live within.
Breathe, so that
it may loosen.

*

Voices within the ark:

Only the
mouths are
safe. You

Sinkenden, hört
auch uns.

*

Keine
Stimme—ein
Spätgeräusch, stundenfremd, deinen
Gedanken geschenkt, hier, endlich
herbeigewacht: ein
Fruchtblatt, augengross, tief
geritzt; es
harzt, will nicht
vernarben.

who sink, listen to
us, too.

*

No
voice—a
late noise, alien to hours, a gift
to your thoughts, here, finally
waking over; a
carpophyll, huge as eyes, deep-
nicked; oozes
resin, won't heal
to a scar.

Zuversicht

Es wird noch ein Aug sein,
ein fremdes, neben
dem unsern: stumm
unter steinernem Lid.

Kommt, bohrt euren Stollen!

Es wird eine Wimper sein,
einwärts gekehrt im Gestein,
von Ungeweintem verstählt,
die feinste der Spindeln.

Vor euch tut sie das Werk,
als gäb es, weil Stein ist, noch Brüder.

Confidence

There will be one more eye,
an alien one, next
to ours: mute
beneath a stone lid.

Come, bore your shaft!

There will be an eyelash—
in-verted in the rock
and tempered by unweptness—
the finest of spindles.

It does the work before you,
as if, because of stone, brothers existed.

Mit Brief und Uhr

Wachs,
Ungeschriebnes zu siegeln,
das deinen Namen
erriet,
das deinen Namen
verschlüsselt.

Kommst du nun, schwimmendes Licht?

Finger, wächsern auch sie,
durch fremde,
schmerzende Ringe gezogen.
Fortgeschmolzen die Kuppen.

Kommst du, schwimmendes Licht?

Zeitleer die Waben der Uhr,
bräutlich das Immentausend,
reisebereit.

Komm, schwimmendes Licht.

With Letter and Clock

Wax,
to seal things unwritten,
divining
your name,
encoding
your name.

Are you coming now, floating light?

Fingers, also waxen,
drawn through
alien, painful rings.
The fingertips, melted away.

Are you coming, floating light?

The clock's honeycombs, time-drained;
nuptial, the bee-myriad,
ready to travel.

Come, floating light.

Unter ein Bild

Rabenüberschwärmte Weizenwoge.
Welchen Himmels Blau? Des untern? Obern?
Später Pfeil, der von der Seele schnellte.
Stärkres Schwirren. Näh'res Glühen. Beide Welten.

Under an Image

Wave of wheat, by ravens overswarmed.
Which sky's blue? The lower sky's? The upper?
Tardy arrow, flying from the soul.
Stronger whizzing. Closer glowing. Both worlds.

Heimkehr

Schneefall, dichter und dichter,
taubenfarben, wie gestern,
Schneefall, als schliefst du auch jetzt noch.

Weithin gelagertes Weiss.
Drüberhin, endlos,
die Schlittenspur des Verlornen.

Darunter, geborgen,
stülpt sich empor,
was den Augen so weh tut,
Hügel um Hügel,
unsichtbar.

Auf jedem,
heimgeholt in sein Heute,
ein ins Stumme entglittenes Ich:
hölzern, ein Pflock.

Dort: ein Gefühl,
vom Eiswind herübergeweht,
das sein tauben-, sein schnee-
farbenes Fahnentuch festmacht.

Homecoming

Snowfall, denser and denser,
dove-colored, like yesterday,
snowfall, as though you still slept.

White, settled far and away.
Above it, endless,
the sleigh-tracks of the lost.

Beneath it, safely sheltered,
what so badly hurts the eyes
tilts upward,
hill by hill,
invisible.

On each one,
brought home into its today,
a self that slipped into dumbness:
wooden, a stake.

There: a feeling
wafted here on the ice-wind,
fastening its dove-colored,
snow-colored flag-cloth.

Unten

Heimgeführt ins Vergessen
das Gast-Gespräch unsrer
langsamen Augen.

Heimgeführt Silbe um Silbe, verteilt
auf die tagblinden Würfel, nach denen
die spielende Hand greift, gross,
im Erwachen.

Und das Zuviel meiner Rede:
angelagert dem kleinen
Kristall in der Tracht deines Schweigens.

Below

Brought home into oblivion,
the guest-talk of our
gradual eyes.

Brought home syllable by syllable, doled out
on the day-blind dice, which
the gambling hand grasps at, huge,
in awakening.

And the overmuch of my speech:
heaping up on the tiny
crystal in the garb of your silence.

Heute und Morgen

So steh ich, steinern, zur
Ferne, in die ich dich führte:

Von Flugsand
ausgewaschen die beiden
Höhlen am untern Stirnsaum.
Eräugtes
Dunkel darin.

Durchpocht
von schweigsam geschwungenen Hämmern
die Stelle,
wo mich das Flügelaug streifte.

Dahinter,
ausgespart in der Wand,
die Stufe,
drauf das Erinnerte hockt.

Hierher
sickert, von Nächten beschenkt,
eine Stimme,
aus der du den Trunk schöpfst.

Today and Tomorrow

Thus I stand, stony, to the
remoteness to which I led you:

Washed out
by driftsand: the two
socket-caves on the lower brow-edge.
Glimpsed
darkness within.

Pounded through
by hammers heaved in hush:
the place
where the wing-eye grazed me.

Behind it,
recessed in the wall,
the step
on which the Remembered squats.

Here,
with gifts from nights, a voice
comes trickling,
from which you drain the draught.

Schliere

Schliere im Aug:
von den Blicken auf halbem
Weg erschautes Verloren.
Wirklichgesponnenes Niemals,
wiedergekehrt.

Wege, halb—und die längsten.

Seelenbeschrittene Fäden,
Glasspur,
rückwärtsgerollt
und nun
vom Augen-Du auf dem steten
Stern über dir
weiss überschleiert.

Schliere im Aug:
dass bewahrt sei
ein durchs Dunkel getragenes Zeichen,
vom Sand (oder Eis?) einer fremden
Zeit für ein fremderes Immer
belebt und als stumm
vibrierender Mitlaut gestimmt.

Streak

Streak in the eye:
lostness beheld at half-
way by the glances.
Real-spun neverness,
returned.

Ways, half—and the longest.

Soul-trodden threads,
glass-trail,
rolled backwards
and now
white-veiled
by the eye-thou on the steady
star above you.

Streak in the eye:
to preserve
a sign borne through the dark,
revived by the sand (or ice?) of
an alien time for a more alien forever
and tuned as a mutely
quivering consonant.

Tenebrae

Nah sind wir, Herr,
nahe und greifbar.

Gegriffen schon, Herr,
ineinander verkrallt, als wär
der Leib eines jeden von uns
dein Leib, Herr.

Bete, Herr,
bete zu uns,
wir sind nah.

Windschief gingen wir hin,
gingen wir hin, uns zu bücken
nach Mulde und Maar.

Zur Tränke gingen wir, Herr.

Es war Blut, es war,
was du vergossen, Herr.

Es glänzte.

Es warf uns dein Bild in die Augen, Herr.
Augen und Mund stehn so offen und leer, Herr.

Wir haben getrunken, Herr.
Das Blut und das Bild, das im Blut war, Herr.

Bete, Herr.
Wir sind nah.

Tenebrae

We are near, Lord,
near and tangible.

Clutched already, Lord,
clawed into one another, as
though each of our bodies were
your body, Lord.

Pray, Lord,
pray to us,
we are near.

Warped, we went there,
went there, to bend over
trough and crater.

We went to the watering-place, Lord.

It was blood, it was
what you had shed, Lord.

It shone.

It cast your image in our eyes, Lord.
Eyes and mouth are so open and blank, Lord.

We have drunk, Lord.
The blood and the image in the blood, Lord.

Pray, Lord.
We are near.

Blume

Der Stein.
Der Stein in der Luft, dem ich folgte.
Dein Aug, so blind wie der Stein.

Wir waren
Hände,
wir schöpften die Finsternis leer, wir fanden
das Wort, das den Sommer heraufkam:
Blume.

Blume—ein Blindenwort.
Dein Aug und mein Aug:
sie sorgen
für Wasser.

Wachstum.
Herzwand um Herzwand
blättert hinzu.

Ein Wort noch, wie dies, und die Hämmer
schwingen im Freien.

Flower

The stone.
The stone in the air, which I followed.
Your eye, as blind as the stone.

We were
hands,
we drained the darkness blank, we found
the word that ascended the summer:
flower.

Flower—a blindman's word.
Your eye and my eye:
they provide
water.

Growth.
Heart-wall by heart-wall
leafs toward it.

One word more, like this one, and the hammers
will heave in the open.

Weiss und Leicht

Sicheldünen, ungezählt.

Im Windschatten, tausendfach: du.
Du und der Arm,
mit dem ich nackt zu dir hinwuchs,
Verlorne.

Die Strahlen. Sie wehn uns zuhauf.
Wir tragen den Schein, den Schmerz und den Namen.

Weiss,
was sich uns regt,
ohne Gewicht,
was wir tauschen.
Weiss und Leicht:
lass es wandern.

Die Fernen, mondnah, wie wir. Sie bauen.
Sie bauen die Klippe, wo
sich das Wandernde bricht,
sie bauen
weiter:
mit Lichtschaum und stäubender Welle.

Das Wandernde, klippenher winkend.
Die Stirnen
winkt es heran,
die Stirnen, die man uns lieh,
um der Spiegelung willen.

White and Weightless

Sickle dunes, unnumbered.

Leeward, myriad: you.
You and the arm
with which I, naked, grew toward you:
the lost one.

The rays. They waft us to heaps.
We bear the glow, the sorrow, and the name.

White
what moves to us,
airy
what we exchange.
White and Weightless:
let it wander.

The distances, moon-near, like us. They build.
They build the reef on which
the Wandering breaks,
they build
on and on:
with light-foam and spraying wave.

The Wandering, beckoning reefward.
It beckons to
the foreheads,
the foreheads we were lent,
for mirroring.

Die Stirnen.
Wir rollen mit ihnen dorthin.
Stirnengestade.

Schläfst du?

Schlaf.

Meermühle geht,
eishell und ungehört,
in unsern Augen.

The foreheads.
We roll there along with them.
Forehead-shores.

Are you sleeping?

Sleep.

Seamill turns,
ice-bright and unheard
in our eyes.

Sprachgitter

Augenrund zwischen den Stäben.

Flimmertier Lid
rudert nach oben,
gibt einen Blick frei.

Iris, Schwimmerin, traumlos und trüb:
der Himmel, herzgrau, muss nah sein.

Schräg, in der eisernen Tülle,
der blakende Span.
Am Lichtsinn
errätst du die Seele.

(Wär ich wie du. Wärst du wie ich.
Standen wir nicht
unter *einem* Passat?
Wir sind Fremde.)

Die Fliesen. Darauf,
dicht beieinander, die beiden
herzgrauen Lachen:
zwei
Mundvoll Schweigen.

Speech-Grille

Eye-orb between the bars.

Ciliary lid
rows upwards,
releases a gaze.

Iris, swimmer, dreamless and dim:
the sky, heart-gray, must be near.

Skew, in the iron socket,
the smoldering splinter.
By the sense of light
you guess the soul.

(Were I like you. Were you like me.
Did we not stand
under *one* tradewind?
We are strangers.)

The tiles. Upon them,
close together, the two
heart-gray pools:
two
mouthfuls of silence.

Schneebett

Augen, weltblind, im Sterbegeklüft: Ich komm,
Hartwuchs im Herzen.
Ich komm.

Mondspiegel Steilwand. Hinab.
(Atemgeflecktes Geleucht. Strichweise Blut.
Wölkende Seele, noch einmal gestaltnah.
Zehnfingerschatten—verklammert.)

Augen weltblind,
Augen im Sterbegeklüft,
Augen Augen:

Das Schneebett unter uns beiden, das Schneebett.
Kristall um Kristall,
zeittief gegittert, wir fallen,
wir fallen und liegen und fallen.

Und fallen:
Wir waren. Wir sind.
Wir sind ein Fleisch mit der Nacht.
In den Gängen, den Gängen.

Snowbed

Eyes, world-blind, in the lode-break of dying: I come,
hard-growth in the heart.
I come.

Moon-mirror precipice. Down.
(Breath-stained light. Scattered blood.
Clouding soul, once again shape-near.
Ten-finger shadow—grappled.)

Eyes world-blind,
eyes in the lode-break of dying,
eyes eyes:

The snowbed beneath us both, the snowbed.
Crystal by crystal,
latticed time-deep, we fall,
we fall and lie and fall.

And fall:
We were. We are.
We are one flesh with the night.
In the lodes, the lodes.

Windgerecht

Tafelwand, grau, mit dem Nachtfries.
Felder, windgerecht, Raute bei Raute,
schriftleer.
Leuchtassel klettert vorbei.

Gesänge:
Augenstimmen, im Chor,
lesen sich wund.
(Ungewesen und Da,
beides zumal,
geht durch die Herzen.)

Später:
Schneewuchs durch alle Gehäuse, frei
ein einziges Feld,
das ein Lichtschein beziffert: die Stimmen.

Die Stimmen:
windgerecht, herznah,
brandbestattet.

Windrowed

Slate-wall, gray, with the night-frieze.
Fields, windrowed, rhomb by rhomb,
with no writing.
Electric centipede climbs past.

Chants:
eye-voices, in chorus,
read themselves sore.
(Never-was and Here,
both at once,
pass through the hearts.)

Later:
snow-growth through all vessels, one
single field is free,
numbered by a radiance: the voices.

The voices:
windrowed, heart-near,
cremated.

Nacht

Kies und Geröll. Und ein Scherbenton, dünn,
als Zuspruch der Stunde.

Augentausch, endlich, zur Unzeit:
bildbeständig,
verholzt
die Netzhaut—:
das Ewigkeitszeichen:

Denkbar:
droben, im Weltgestänge,
sterngleich,
das Rot zweier Münder.

Hörbar (vor Morgen?): ein Stein,
der den andern zum Ziel nahm.

Night

Gravel and rubble. And a shard-tone, thin,
as the hour's solace.

Barter of eyes, finite, untimely:
image-steady,
wooden
the retina—:
the sign of eternity.

Conceivable:
up there, in the world-rods,
star-like,
the red of two mouths.

Audible (by morning?): a stone
that made the other a target.

Matière de Bretagne

Ginsterlicht, gelb, die Hänge
eitern gen Himmel, der Dorn
wirbt um die Wunde, es läutet
darin, es ist Abend, das Nichts
rollt seine Meere zur Andacht,
das Blutsegel hält auf dich zu.

Trocken, verlandet
das Bett hinter dir, verschilft
seine Stunde, oben,
beim Stern, die milchigen
Priele schwatzen im Schlamm, Steindattel,
unten, gebuscht, klafft ins Gebläu, eine Staude
Vergänglichkeit, schön,
grüsst dein Gedächtnis.

(Kanntet ihr mich,
Hände? Ich ging
den gegabelten Weg, den ihr wiest, mein Mund
spie seinen Schotter, ich ging, meine Zeit,
wandernde Wächte, warf ihren Schatten—kanntet ihr mich?)

Hände, die dorn-
umworbene Wunde, es läutet,
Hände, das Nichts, seine Meere,
Hände, im Ginsterlicht, das
Blutsegel
hält auf dich zu.

Matière de Bretagne

Furze-light, yellow, the slopes
fester skywards, the thorn
woos the wound, a knell tolls
within, it is evening, the void
rolls its seas to devotion,
the blood-sail steers at you.

Arid, aground,
the bed behind you, sedge-choked
its hour, above,
at the star, the milky
narrows chatter in mud, stone-borer,
below, bushy, gapes into blueness, a shrub of
ephemeralness, lovely,
hails your memory.

(Did you know me,
hands? I followed
the forking road you showed me, my mouth
spit out its chippings, I walked, my time,
a wandering snow-wall, cast its shadow—did you know me?)

Hands, the thorn-
wooed wound, a knell,
hands, the void, its seas,
hands, in the furze-light, the
blood-sail
steers at you.

Du
du lehrst
du lehrst deine Hände
du lehrst deine Hände du lehrst
du lehrst deine Hände
                    schlafen

You
you teach
you teach your hands
you teach your hands you teach
you teach your hands
                    to sleep

Schuttkahn

Wasserstunde, der Schuttkahn
fährt uns zu Abend, wir haben,
wie er, keine Eile, ein totes
Warum steht am Heck.

. . . .

Geleichtert. Die Lunge, die Qualle
bläht sich zur Glocke, ein brauner
Seelenfortsatz erreicht
das hellgeatmete Nein.

Rubble-Boat

Water-hour, the rubble-boat
takes us toward evening, we are,
like it, in no hurry, a dead
Why stands astern.

. . . .

Lightened. The lung, the jellyfish
bloats up into a bell, a brown
soul-appendage reaches
the brightly-breathed No.

Köln, Am Hof

Herzzeit, es stehn
die Geträumten für
die Mitternachtsziffer.

Einiges sprach in die Stille, einiges schwieg,
einiges ging seiner Wege.
Verbannt und Verloren
waren daheim.

Ihr Dome.

Ihr Dome ungesehn,
ihr Ströme unbelauscht,
ihr Uhren tief in uns.

Cologne, Am Hof

Heart-time, the dreamt
stand for the
midnight digit.

Some spoke into stillness, some remained silent,
some went its way.
Exiled and Lost
were at home.

You cathedrals.

You cathedrals unseen,
you rivers unheard,
you clocks deep within us.

In die Ferne

Stummheit, aufs neue, geräumig, ein Haus—:
komm, du sollst wohnen.

Stunden, fluchschön gestuft: erreichbar
die Freistatt.

Schärfer als je die verbliebene Luft: du sollst atmen,
atmen und du sein.

Into the Distance

Muteness, again, spacious, a house—:
come, you shall dwell.

Hours, gradated curse-lovely: attainable
the sanctuary.

The remaining air, ranker than ever: you shall breathe,
breathe and be you.

Ein Tag und Noch Einer

Föhniges Du. Die Stille
flog uns voraus, ein zweites,
deutliches Leben.

Ich gewann, ich verlor, wir glaubten
an düstere Wunder, der Ast,
rasch an den Himmel geschrieben, trug uns, wuchs
durchs ziehende Weiss in die Mondbahn, ein Morgen
sprang ins Gestern hinauf, wir holten,
zerstoben, den Leuchter, ich stürzte
alles in niemandes Hand.

A Day and One More

Foehn-like you. The stillness
flew ahead of us, a second,
distinct life.

I won, I lost, we believed
in somber wonders, the branch,
hastily scrawled on the sky, carried us, grew
through drifting white into moon-orbit, a tomorrow
leaped up into yesterday, we brought
the pulverized candlestick, I dumped
everything into no one's hand.

In Mundhöhe

In Mundhöhe, fühlbar:
Finstergewächs.

(Brauchst es, Licht, nicht zu suchen, bleibst
das Schneegarn, hältst
deine Beute.

Beides gilt:
Berührt und Unberührt.
Beides spricht mit der Schuld von der Liebe,
beides will dasein und sterben.)

Blattnarben, Knospen, Gewimper.
Äugendes, tagfremd.
Schelfe, wahr und offen.

Lippe wusste. Lippe weiss.
Lippe schweigt es zu Ende.

On Mouth-Level

On mouth-level, palpable:
dark-growth.

(Light, you need not seek it, you remain
the snow-snare, you hold
your prey.

Both are valid:
Touched and Untouched.
Both speak with guilt about love,
both want to be and die.)

Leaf-scars, buds, ciliation.
A glimpsing, alien to day.
Husk, true and open.

Lip knew. Lip knows.
Lip dumbs it to the end.

Eine Hand

Der Tisch, aus Stundenholz, mit
dem Reisgericht und dem Wein.
Es wird
geschwiegen, gegessen, getrunken.

Eine Hand, die ich küsste,
leuchtet den Mündern.

A Hand

The table, of hour-wood, with
the rice-dish and the wine.
There is
silence, eating, drinking.

A hand that I kissed
lights the way for the mouths.

Aber

(Du
fragst ja, ich
sags dir:)

Strahlengang, immer, die
Spiegel, nachtweit, stehn
gegeneinander, ich bin,
hingestossen zu dir, eines
Sinnes mit diesem
Vorbei.

Aber: mein Herz
ging durch die Pause, es wünscht dir
das Aug, bildnah und zeitstark,
das mich verformt—:

die Schwäne,
in Genf, ich sah's nicht, flogen, es war,
als schwirrte, vom Nichts her, ein Wurfholz
ins Ziel einer Seele: soviel
Zeit
denk mir, als Auge, jetzt zu:
dass ichs
schwirren hör, näher—nicht
neben mir, nicht,
wo du nicht sein kannst.

But

(You
do ask, I
tell you:)

Corridor of rays, always, the
mirrors, night-far, stand
face to face, I,
joining you, am of one
mind with this
Done-with.

But: my heart
passed through the pause, it wishes you
the eye, image-near and time-strong,
that misshapes me—:

the swans,
in Geneva, I didn't see them, flew
as if, from the void, a javelin were whizzing
into a soul's target: focus
so much
time, as an eye, at me, now:
so that I
may hear it whiz, nearer—not
next to me, not
where you cannot be.

Allerseelen

Was hab ich
getan?
Die Nacht besamt, als könnt es
noch andere geben, nächtiger als
diese.

Vogelflug, Steinflug, tausend
beschriebene Bahnen. Blicke,
geraubt und gepflückt. Das Meer,
gekostet, vertrunken, verträumt. Eine Stunde,
seelenverfinstert. Die nächste, ein Herbstlicht,
dargebracht einem blinden
Gefühl, das des Wegs kam. Andere, viele,
ortlos und schwer aus sich selbst: erblickt und umgangen.
Findlinge, Sterne,
schwarz und voll Sprache: benannt
nach zerschwiegenem Schwur.

Und einmal (wann? auch dies ist vergessen):
den Widerhaken gefühlt,
wo der Puls den Gegentakt wagte.

All Souls

What have I
done?
Inseminated the night, as if
more might exist, nightlier
still.

Birdflight, stone-flight, a thousand
described paths. Gazes,
raped and culled. The sea,
tasted, drunk dry, dreamt away. One hour,
soul-eclipsed. The next, an autumn-light,
offered up to a blind
feeling, which came this way. Others, many,
placeless and heavy of themselves: sighted and shunned.
Foundlings, stars,
black and speech-filled: named
for an oath hushed to bits.

And once (when? this too is forgotten):
felt the barb
where the pulse hazarded counter-beat.

Entwurf einer Landschaft

Rundgräber, unten. Im
Viertakt der Jahresschritt auf
den Steilstufen rings.

Laven, Basalte, weltherz-
durchglühtes Gestein.
Quelltuff,
wo uns das Licht wuchs, vor
dem Atem.

Ölgrün, meerdurchstäubt die
unbetretbare Stunde. Gegen
die Mitte zu, grau,
ein Steinsattel, drauf,
gebeult und verkohlt,
die Tierstirn mit
der strahligen Blesse.

Draft of a Landscape

Round-graves, below. In
four-time the year-pace on
the steep-steps all around.

Lavas, basalts, worldheart-
heated stone.
Source-tuff,
where light grew for us, before
breath.

Oil-green, thoroughly sea-sprayed the
inaccessible hour. Towards
the center, gray,
a stone-ridge, on it,
dented and charred,
the animal-brow with
the radiant blaze.

Ein Auge, Offen

Stunden, maifarben, kühl.
Das nicht mehr zu Nennende, heiss,
hörbar im Mund.

Niemandes Stimme, wieder.

Schmerzende Augapfeltiefe:
das Lid
steht nicht im Wege, die Wimper
zählt nicht, was eintritt.

Die Träne, halb,
die schärfere Linse, beweglich,
holt dir die Bilder.

One Eye, Open

Hours, May-colored, cool.
The No-longer-nameable, hot,
audible in the mouth.

No one's voice, again.

Painful eyeball-depth:
the lid
is not in the way, the lashes
do not count what enters.

The tear, half,
the keener lens, mobile,
brings you the images.

Oben, geräuschlos, die
Fahrenden: Geier und Stern.

Unten, nach allem, wir,
zehn an der Zahl, das Sandvolk. Die Zeit,
wie denn auch nicht, sie hat
auch für uns eine Stunde, hier,
in der Sandstadt.

(Erzähl von den Brunnen, erzähl
von Brunnenkranz, Brunnenrad, von
Brunnenstuben—erzähl.

Zähl und erzähl, die Uhr,
auch diese, läuft ab.

Wasser: welch
ein Wort. Wir verstehen dich, Leben.)

Der Fremde, ungebeten, woher,
der Gast.
Sein triefendes Kleid.
Sein triefendes Auge.

(Erzähl uns von Brunnen, von—
Zähl und erzähl.
Wasser: welch
ein Wort.)

Sein Kleid-und-Auge, er steht,
wie wir, voller Nacht, er bekundet

Above, noiseless, the
travelers: vulture and star.

Below, after everything, we,
tallying ten, the sand-folk. Time,
why shouldn't it, has
an hour for us too, here,
in the sand-city.

(Tell about the wells, tell
about the well-wreath, well-wheel, the
well-rooms—tell.

Tally and tell, the clock,
even this one, runs down.

Water: what
a word. We understand you, life.)

The stranger, uninvited, from where,
the guest.
His dripping robe.
His dripping eye.

(Tell us about wells, about—
Tally and tell.
Water: what
a word.)

His robe-and-eye, he stands,
like us, full of night, he manifests

Einsicht, er zählt jetzt,
wie wir, bis zehn
und nicht weiter.

Oben, die
Fahrenden
bleiben
unhörbar.

discernment, he's counting now
as we do till ten
and no further.

Above, the
travelers
remain
inaudible.

Die Welt, zu uns
in die leere Stunde getreten:

Zwei
Baumschäfte, schwarz,
unverzweigt, ohne
Knoten.
In der Düsenspur, scharfrandig, das
eine frei-
stehende Hochblatt.

Auch wir hier, im Leeren,
stehn bei den Fahnen.

The world, coming
to us into the empty hour:

Two
tree-trunks, black,
non-ramose, without
knots.
In the jet's trail, sharp-edged, the
one in-
adherent bract.

We too here, in emptiness,
stand by the banners.

Ein Holzstern, blau,
aus kleinen Rauten gebaut. Heute, von
der jüngsten unserer Hände.

Das Wort, während
du Salz aus der Nacht fällst, der Blick
wieder die Windgalle sucht:

—Ein Stern, tu ihn,
tu den Stern in die Nacht.

(—In meine, in
meine.)

A woodstar, blue,
built of small rhombs. Today, by
the youngest of our hands.

The word, while
you fell salt from the night, and the gaze
again seeks the oxeye:

—A star, put it,
put the star in the night.

(—In mine, in
mine.)

Sommerbericht

Der nicht mehr beschrittene, der
umgangene Thymianteppich.
Eine Leerzeile, quer
durch die Glockenheide gelegt.
Nichts in den Windbruch getragen.

Wieder Begegnungen mit
vereinzelten Worten wie:
Steinschlag, Hartgräser, Zeit.

Summer Report

The no longer trodden, the
shunned thyme-carpet.
A blank-line, slanting
through the erica. Nothingness
borne into the windfalls.

Again encounters with
isolate words like:
macadam, fescues, time.

Niedrigwasser. Wir sahen
die Seepocke, sahen
die Napfschnecke, sahen
die Nägel an unsern Händen.
Niemand schnitt uns das Wort von der Herzwand.

(Fährten der Strandkrabbe, morgen,
Kriechfurchen, Wohngänge, Wind-
zeichnung im grauen
Schlick. Feinsand,
Grobsand, das
von den Wänden Gelöste, bei
andern Hartteilen, im
Schill.)

Ein Aug, heute,
gab es dem zweiten, beide,
geschlossen, folgten der Strömung zu
ihrem Schatten, setzten
die Fracht ab (*niemand
schnitt uns das Wort von der*—), bauten
den Haken hinaus—eine Nehrung, vor
ein kleines
unbefahrbares Schweigen.

Low-water. We saw
the sea-acorn, saw
the cunner, saw
the nails on our hands.
No one cut the word from our heart-walls.

(Spoors of the shore-crab, tomorrow,
scuttle-furrows, lair-burrows, wind-
sketch in the gray
slime. Fine sand,
coarse sand, loosened
from the walls, by
other hard-parts, in the
perch-pike.)

One eye, today,
gave it to the second, both,
closed, followed the current to
their shadow, discharged
the freight (*no one*
cut the word from our—), built
out the hook—a landtongue, before
a tiny
unnavigable silence.

Bahndämme, Wegränder, Ödplätze, Schutt

Lichtgewinn, messbar, aus
Distelähnlichem:
einiges
Rot, im Gespräch
mit einigem Gelb.
Die Luftschleier vor
deinem verzweifelten Aug.
Das letzte
reitende Sandkorn.

(Die
Augärten, damals, das
gelächelte Wort
vom Marchfeld, vom
Steppengras dort.
Das tote Ringelspiel, kling.
Wir
drehten uns weiter.)

Der Sandkornritt, das
Auge, ihm zugewandt.
Die Stundentür und
ihre Geräusche.

Train-Tracks, Roadsides, Vacant Lots, Rubble

Light-gain, gaugeable, from
something thistle-like:
some
red, conversing
with some yellow.
The air-films before
your desperate eye.
The last
equitant sand-grain.

(The
Augartens,* in those days, the
smiled word
about the Marchfeld, the
steppe-grass there.
The dead merry-go-round, ding.
We
kept revolving.)

The sand-grain ride, the
eye, turned towards it.
The hour-door and
its noises.

* Notes appear on p. 254.

Engführung

*

Verbracht ins
Gelände
mit der untrüglichen Spur:

Gras, auseinandergeschrieben. Die Steine, weiss,
mit den Schatten der Halme:
Lies nicht mehr—schau!
Schau nicht mehr—geh!

Geh, deine Stunde
hat keine Schwestern, du bist—
bist zuhause. Ein Rad, langsam,
rollt aus sich selber, die Speichen
klettern,
klettern auf schwärzlichem Feld, die Nacht
braucht keine Sterne, nirgends
fragt es nach dir.

*

               Nirgends
                    fragt es nach dir—

Der Ort, wo sie lagen, er hat
einen Namen—er hat
keinen. Sie lagen nicht dort. Etwas
lag zwischen ihnen. Sie
sahn nicht hindurch.

154

Stretto

*

Brought to
the area
with the unerring trail:

grass, written apart. The stones, white,
with the shadows of blades:
Read no more—watch!
Watch no more—walk!

Walk, your hour
has no sisters, you are—
are at home. A wheel, slow,
rolls on its own, the spokes
climb,
climb up a blackish expanse, the night
needs no stars, no asking
for you anywhere.

*

                          No asking
                                    for you anywhere—

The place where they lay, it has
a name—it has
none. They did not lie there. Something
lay between them. They
could not see through.

Sahn nicht, nein,
redeten von
Worten. Keines
erwachte, der
Schlaf
kam über sie.

*

                              Kam, kam. Nirgends
                                       fragt es—

Ich bins, ich,
ich lag zwischen euch, ich war
offen, war
hörbar, ich tickte euch zu, euer Atem
gehorchte, ich
bin es noch immer, ihr
schlaft ja.

*

                              Bin es noch immer—

Jahre.
Jahre, Jahre, ein Finger
tastet hinab und hinan, tastet
umher:
Nahtstellen, fühlbar, hier
klafft es weit auseinander, hier
wuchs es wieder zusammen—wer
deckte es zu?

*

                              Deckte es
                                  zu—wer?

156

Could not see, no,
spoke of
words. None
awoke,
sleep
came over them.

*

                                        Came, came. No
                                                asking—

It's I, I,
I lay among you, I was
open, was
audible, I ticked toward you, your breath
obeyed, I'm
still the same, but you
are sleeping.

*

                                             Still the same—

Years.
Years, years, a finger
gropes down and up, gropes
about:
Seams, palpable, here
a yawning gap, here
it grew together again—who
covered it up?

*

                                            Covered it
                                                up—who?

Kam, kam.
Kam ein Wort, kam,
kam durch die Nacht,
wollt leuchten, wollt leuchten.

Asche.
Asche, Asche.
Nacht.
Nacht-und-Nacht.—Zum
Aug geh, zum feuchten.

*

                    Zum
                        Aug geh,
                                zum feuchten—

Orkane.
Orkane, von je,
Partikelgestöber, das andre,
du
weissts ja, wir
lasens im Buche, war
Meinung.

War, war
Meinung. Wie
fassten wir uns
an—an mit
diesen
Händen?

Es stand auch geschrieben, dass.
Wo? Wir
taten ein Schweigen darüber,
giftgestillt, gross,

Came, came.
Came a word, came,
came through the night,
wanted to glow, to glow.

Ashes.
Ashes, ashes.
Night.
Night-and-night. —Go
to the eye, the moist one.

*

                              Go
                        to the eye,
                                  the moist one—

Hurricanes.
Hurricanes, ever since always,
Particle flurries, the other,
you
know, we
read it in the book, it was
opinion.

Was, was
opinion. How
did we take hands
—take hands with
these
hands?

And it was written that.
Where? We
passed a silence over it,
venom-sated, huge

ein
grünes
Schweigen, ein Kelchblatt, es
hing ein Gedanke an Pflanzliches dran—
grün, ja,
hing, ja,
unter hämischem
Himmel.

An, ja,
Pflanzliches.

Ja.
Orkane, Par-
tikelgestöber, es blieb
Zeit, blieb,
es beim Stein zu versuchen—er
war gastlich, er
fiel nicht ins Wort. Wie
gut wir es hatten:

Körnig,
körnig und faserig. Stengelig,
dicht;
traubig und strahlig; nierig,
plattig und
klumpig; locker, ver-
ästelt—: er, es
fiel nicht ins Wort, es
sprach,
sprach gerne zu trockenen Augen, eh es sie schloss.

Sprach, sprach.
War, war.

Wir
liessen nicht locker, standen

a
green
silence, a sepal, a
thought of plant clung to it—
green, yes,
clung, yes,
below a spiteful
sky.

Of, yes,
plant.

Yes.
Hurricanes, par-
ticle flurries, there was still
time, time
to try it at the stone—it
was hospitable, it
never abrupted. How
well off we were:

Grainy,
grainy and fibrous. Stalked,
dense:
clustery and radial; renal,
lamellated and
rugged; loose, ram-
ified—; it, it
never abrupted, it
spoke,
spoke readily to dry eyes, before closing them.

Spoke, spoke.
Was, was.

We
wouldn't give in, we stood

inmitten, ein
Porenbau, und
es kam.

Kam auf uns zu, kam
hindurch, flickte
unsichtbar, flickte
an der letzten Membran,
und
die Welt, ein Tausendkristall,
schoss an, schoss an.

*

Schoss an, schoss an.
Dann—

Nächte, entmischt. Kreise,
grün oder blau, rote
Quadrate: die
Welt setzt ihr Innerstes ein
im Spiel mit den neuen
Stunden.—Kreise,
rot oder schwarz, helle
Quadrate, kein
Flugschatten,
kein
Messtisch, keine
Rauchseele steigt und spielt mit.

*

Steigt und
spielt mit—

In der Eulenflucht, beim
versteinerten Aussatz,

in the middle, a
structure of pores, and
it came.

Came towards us, came
through, mended
invisibly, mended
the last membrane,
and the world, a myriad crystal,
shot, shot.

        *

                                        Shot, shot.
                                              Then—

nights, decomposed. Circles,
green or blue, red
squares: the
world stakes its innermost in
the game with the new
hours.—Circles,
red or black, bright
squares, no
flight-shadow,
no
surveyor's table, no
smoke-soul rises and joins in.

        *

                                   Rises and
                                        joins in—

In the owl-light, by the
petrified leprosy,

bei
unsern geflohenen Händen, in
der jüngsten Verwerfung,
überm
Kugelfang an
der verschütteten Mauer:

sichtbar, aufs
neue: die
Rillen, die

Chöre, damals, die
Psalmen. Ho, ho-
sianna.

Also
stehen noch Tempel. Ein
Stern
hat wohl noch Licht.
Nichts,
nichts ist verloren.

Ho-
sianna.

In der Eulenflucht, hier,
die Gespräche, taggrau,
der Grundwasserspuren.

*

                     (—taggrau,
                           der
                                Grundwasserspuren—

Verbracht
ins Gelände

by
our fled hands, in
the most recent dislocation
above
the shooting-butt at
the demolished wall.

visible, once
more the
grooves, the

choirs, back then, the
psalms. Ho, ho-
sanna.

And so
temples still stand. A
star
may still have light.
Nothing,
nothing is lost.

Ho-
sanna.

In the owl-light, here,
the talking, dawn-gray,
of groundwater trails.

*

(—dawn-gray,
of
groundwater trails.

Brought to
the area

mit
der untrüglichen
Spur:

Gras.
Gras,
auseinandergeschrieben.)

with
the unerring
trail:

Grass.
Grass,
written apart.)

aus
Die Niemandsrose

from
The No-One's-Rose

Soviel Gestirne, die
man uns hinhält. Ich war,
als ich dich ansah—wann?—,
draussen bei
den andern Welten.

O diese Wege, galaktisch,
o diese Stunde, die uns
die Nächte herüberwog in
die Last unsrer Namen. Es ist,
ich weiss es, nicht wahr,
dass wir lebten, es ging
blind nur ein Atem zwischen
Dort und Nicht-da und Zuweilen,
kometenhaft schwirrte ein Aug
auf Erloschenes zu, in den Schluchten,
da, wo's verglühte, stand
zitzenprächtig die Zeit,
an der schon empor- und hinab-
und hinwegwuchs, was
ist oder war oder sein wird—,

ich weiss,
ich weiss und du weisst, wir wussten,
wir wussten nicht, wir
waren ja da und nicht dort,
und zuweilen, wenn
nur das Nichts zwischen uns stand, fanden
wir ganz zueinander.

So many stars held
out to us. I was
when I gazed at you—when?—
outside at
the other worlds.

Oh these roads, galactic,
oh this hour that
the nights weighed over to us
to the charge of our names. It is,
I know, not true
that we lived, it was
simply a breath passing blindly
between There and Not-Here and At-Times,
comet-like an eye whizzed
towards snuffed things, in the canyons,
there where it glowed out, stood
richly-teated time,
on which there already grew up
and down and beyond, what
is or was or will be—

I know,
I know and you know, we knew,
we did not know, we
were here after all and not there,
and at times, when
only the void stood between us, we
found our full ways to each other.

Es war Erde in ihnen, und
sie gruben.

Sie gruben und gruben, so ging
ihr Tag dahin, ihre Nacht. Und sie lobten nicht Gott,
der, so hörten sie, alles dies wollte,
der, so hörten sie, alles dies wusste.

Sie gruben und hörten nichts mehr;
sie wurden nicht weise, erfanden kein Lied,
erdachten sich keinerlei Sprache.
Sie gruben.

Es kam eine Stille, es kam auch ein Sturm,
es kamen die Meere alle.
Ich grabe, du gräbst, und es gräbt auch der Wurm,
und das Singende dort sagt: Sie graben.

O einer, o keiner, o niemand, o du:
Wohin gings, da's nirgendhin ging?
O du gräbst und ich grab, und ich grab mich dir zu,
und am Finger erwacht uns der Ring.

There was earth in them, and
they dug.

They dug and dug, and thus
their day wore on, and their night. And they did not praise God,
who, they heard, willed all this,
who, they heard, knew all this.

They dug and heard no more;
they did not grow wise, nor contrive any song,
or any kind of language.
They dug.

There came a stillness, and there came a storm,
and all the oceans came.
I dig, you dig, and the worm digs too,
and the singing there says: they dig.

Oh someone, oh none, oh no one, oh you:
Where did it go, if nowhere it went.
Oh you dig and I dig, and to you I dig in,
and the ring awakes on our fingers.

Das Wort vom Zur-Tiefe-Gehn,
das wir gelesen haben.
Die Jahre, die Worte seither.
Wir sind es noch immer.

Weisst du, der Raum ist unendlich,
weisst du, du brauchst nicht zu fliegen,
weisst du, was sich in dein Aug schrieb,
vertieft uns die Tiefe.

The word of going-to-the-depth,
which we once read.
The years, the words ever since.
We are still the same.

You know, space is unending,
you know, you don't have to fly,
you know, what wrote itself into your eye
deepens the depth for us.

Bei Wein und Verlorenheit, bei
beider Neige:

ich ritt durch den Schnee, hörst du,
ich ritt Gott in die Ferne—die Nähe, er sang,
es war
unser lezter Ritt über
die Menschen-Hürden.

Sie duckten sich, wenn
sie uns über sich hörten, sie
schrieben, sie
logen unser Gewieher
um in eine
ihrer bebilderten Sprachen.

By wine and lostness, by
the lees of both:

I rode through the snow, do you hear,
I rode God far—and near, he sang,
it was
our last ride over
the human-hurdles.

They cowered when
they heard us overhead, they
rewrote, they
lied our whinnying
into one
of their illustrated languages.

Zürich, Zum Storchen

Für Nelly Sachs

Vom Zuviel war die Rede, vom
Zuwenig. Von Du
und Aber-Du, von
der Trübung durch Helles, von
Jüdischem, von
deinem Gott.

Da-
von.
Am Tag einer Himmelfahrt, das
Münster stand drüben, es kam
mit einigem Gold übers Wasser.

Von deinem Gott war die Rede, ich sprach
gegen ihn, ich
liess das Herz, das ich hatte,
hoffen:
auf
sein höchstes, umröcheltes, sein
haderndes Wort—

Dein Aug sah mir zu, sah hinweg,
dein Mund
sprach sich dem Aug zu, ich hörte:

Wir
wissen ja nicht, weisst du,
wir
wissen ja nicht,
was
gilt.

Zurich, Zum Storchen

For Nelly Sachs

The talk was of too much, too
little. Of Thou
and thou again, of
the dimming through light, of
Jewishness, of
your God.

Of
that.
On the day of an ascension, the
cathedral stood on the other side, it passed
over the water with some gold.

The talk was of your God, I spoke
against Him, I
let the heart that I had,
hope:
for His highest, His deathrattled, His
angry word—

Your eye looked at me, looked away,
your mouth
spoke to your eye, I heard:

We
simply do not know, you know,
we
simply do not know
what
counts.

Die Schleuse

Über aller dieser deiner
Trauer: kein
zweiter Himmel.

.   .   .   .

An einen Mund,
dem es ein Tausendwort war,
verlor—
verlor ich ein Wort,
das mir verblieben war:
Schwester.

An
die Vielgötterei
verlor ich ein Wort, das mich suchte:
Kaddisch.

Durch
die Schleuse musst ich,
das Wort in die Salzflut zurück-
und hinaus- und hinüberzuretten:
Jiskor.

The Sluice

Over all this grief of
yours: no
second heaven.

. . . .

To a mouth,
for which it was a myriad-word,
I lost—
lost a word
left over for me:
sister.

To
many-godded-ness
I lost a word that sought me:
*Kaddish.**

Through
the sluice I had to go,
to save the word back into,
and across, and beyond the brine:
*Yiskor **

Psalm

Niemand knetet uns wieder aus Erde und Lehm,
niemand bespricht unsern Staub.
Niemand.

Gelobt seist du, Niemand.
Dir zulieb wollen
wir blühn.
Dir
entgegen.

Ein Nichts
waren wir, sind wir, werden
wir bleiben, blühend:
die Nichts-, die
Niemandsrose.

Mit
dem Griffel seelenhell,
dem Staubfaden himmelswüst,
der Krone rot
vom Purpurwort, das wir sangen
über, o über
dem Dorn.

Psalm

No one kneads us again of earth and clay,
no one incants our dust.
No one.

Blessed art thou, No-one.
For thy sake we
will bloom.
Towards
thee.

We were, we are, we shall remain
a Nothing,
blooming:
the Nothing-, the
No-one's-Rose.

With
the style soul-bright,
the filament heaven-void,
the corolla red
from the purple word that we sang
over, oh over
the thorn.

Tübingen, Jänner

Zur Blindheit über-
redete Augen.
Ihre—» ein
Rätsel ist Rein-
entsprungenes«—, ihre
Erinnerung an
schwimmende Hölderlintürme, möwen-
umschwirrt.

Besuche ertrunkener Schreiner bei
diesen
tauchenden Worten:

Käme,
käme ein Mensch,
käme ein Mensch zur Welt, heute, mit
dem Lichtbart der
Patriarchen: er dürfte,
spräch er von dieser
Zeit, er
dürfte
nur lallen und lallen,
immer-, immer-
zuzu.

(»Pallaksch. Pallaksch.«)

Tübingen, January

Eyes, talked
into blindness.
Their ("pure
origin is an
enigma"), their
memory of
floating Hölderlin Towers, circled
by whirring gulls.

Visits of drowned carpenters to
these
submerging words:

If there came,
came a man,
came a man to the world, today, with
the bright beard of the
patriarchs: he could,
if he spoke of these
times, he
could
only st-utter, stutter,
all, all ways, al-
ways.

("Pallaksch. Pallaksch.")

Chymisch

Schweigen, wie Gold gekocht, in
verkohlten
Händen.

Grosse, graue,
wie alles Verlorene nahe
Schwestergestalt:

Alle die Namen, alle die mit-
verbrannten
Namen. Soviel
zu segnende Asche. Soviel
gewonnenes Land
über
den leichten, so leichten
Seelen-
ringen.

Grosse. Graue. Schlacken-
lose.

Du, damals.
Du mit der fahlen,
aufgebissenen Knospe.
Du in der Weinflut.

(Nicht wahr, auch uns
entliess diese Uhr?

Gut,
gut, wie dein Wort hier vorbeistarb.)

Chymical

Silence, boiled like gold, in
charred
hands.

Large, gray
sister-shape,
near as all that's lost:

All the names, all the
names cremated
along. So many
ashes to bless. So much
land gained
above
the weightless, so weightless
soul-
rings.

Large. Gray. Slag-
less.

You, then.
You with the wan
bud bitten open.
You in the wine-flood.

(Isn't it so, this clock
released us, too?

Good,
good, that your word died past here.)

Schweigen, wie Gold gekocht, in
verkohlten, verkohlten
Händen.
Finger, rauchdünn. Wie Kronen, Luftkronen
um—

Grosse. Graue. Fährte-
lose.
Königliche.
Königliche.

Silence, boiled like gold, in
charred, charred
hands.
Fingers, smoke-thin. Like crowns, air-crowns
around—

Large. Gray. Spoor-
less.
Royal
one.

Es ist nicht mehr
diese
zuweilen mit dir
in die Stunde gesenkte
Schwere. Es ist
eine andre.

Es ist das Gewicht, das die Leere zurückhält,
die mit-
ginge mit dir.
Es hat, wie du, keinen Namen. Vielleicht
seid ihr dasselbe. Vielleicht
nennst auch du mich einst
so.

It is no longer
this
heaviness sometimes
sunken with you in
the hour. It is
a different one.

It is the weight that holds back the vacuum
that would
go with you.
It has, like you, no name. Perhaps
you are both *one*. Perhaps
some day you too will name me
thus.

Zweihäusig, Ewiger, bist du, un-
bewohnbar. Darum
baun wir und bauen. Darum
steht sie, diese
erbärmliche Bettstatt, —im Regen,
da steht sie.

Komm, Geliebte.
Dass wir hier liegen, das
ist die Zwischenwand—: Er
hat dann genug an sich selber, zweimal.

Lass ihn, er
habe sich ganz, als das Halbe
und abermals Halbe. Wir,
wir sind das Regenbett, er
komme und lege uns trocken.

. . . .

Er kommt nicht, er legt uns nicht trocken.

Dioecious,* Eternal One, art thou, un-
inhabitable. Therefore
we build and build. Therefore
it stands, this
woeful bedstead—in the rain,
there it stands.

Come, beloved.
That we may lie here, this
is the partition—: He
thus has enough in himself, twice.

Let him, may he
have himself wholly, as the half
and the half again. We,
we are the rainbed, may he
come and drain us.

. . . .

He won't come, he won't drain us.

Sibirisch

Bogengebete—du
sprachst sie nicht mit, es waren,
du denkst es, die deinen.

Der Rabenschwan hing
vorm frühen Gestirn:
mit zerfressenem Lidspalt
stand ein Gesicht—auch unter diesem
Schatten.

Kleine, im Eiswind
liegengebliebene
Schelle
mit deinem
weissen Kiesel im Mund:

Auch mir
steht der tausendjahrfarbene
Stein in der Kehle, der Herzstein,
auch ich
setze Grünspan an
an der Lippe.

Über die Schuttflur hier,
durch das Seggenmeer heute
führt sie, unsre
Bronze-Strasse.
Da lieg ich und rede zu dir
mit abgehäutetem
Finger.

Siberian

Arc-prayers—you
did not speak them along, they were
(you think) yours.

The raven-swan hung
before the early star:
with a corroded lid-cleft
a face stood—under this
shadow too.

Small bell
left lying in the
polar wind
with your
white pebble in your mouth:

I, too,
have the millennium-colored
stone in my throat, the heart-stone;
I, too,
gather verdigris
on my lip.

Across the rubble-field here,
through the sedge-sea today,
it runs, our
bronze-highway.
Here I lie and speak to you
with a flayed
finger.

Benedicta

Zu ken men arojfgejn in himel arajn
Un fregn baj got zu's darf asoj sajn?

Jiddisches Lied

Ge-
truken hast du,
was von den Vätern mir kam
und von jenseits der Väter:
—Pneuma.

Ge-
segnet seist du, von weit her, von
jenseits meiner
erloschenen Finger.

Gesegnet: Du, die ihn grüsste,
den Teneberleuchter.

Du, die du's hörtest, da ich die Augen schloss, wie
die Stimme nicht weitersang nach:
's mus asoj sajn.

Du, die du's sprachst in den augen-
losen, den Auen:
dasselbe, das andere
Wort:
Gebenedeiet.

Ge-
trunken.
Ge-
segnet.
Ge-
bentscht.

Benedicta

Tsu ken men aroifgeyn in himel arayn
Un fregn bai got tsu's darf azoy sayn?

Can you go up to heaven and say
God, is it meant to be this way?

—Yiddish song

Drunk
you have drunk
what came to me from our fathers
and from beyond our fathers:
—Pneuma.

Blessed
art thou, from afar, from
beyond my
defunct fingers.

Blessed: you who greeted them,
the teneber tapers.

You who heard, when I closed my eyes,
the voice stop singing after:
it must be this way.

You who spoke it in the eye-
less ones, the meadows:
the same, the different
word:
gebenedeiet.

Drunk.
Blessed.
*Gebentsht.**

Hawdalah

An dem einen, dem
einzigen
Faden, an ihm
spinnst du—von ihm
Umsponnener, ins
Freie, dahin,
ins Gebundne.

Gross
stehn die Spindeln
ins Unland, die Bäume: es ist,
von unten her, ein
Licht geknüpft in die Luft-
matte, auf der du den Tisch deckst, den leeren
Stühlen und ihrem
Sabbatglanz zu—

zu Ehren.

Havdalah *

On the one, the
only
thread, you
spin on it—spun round
by it, into
freeness, there,
into boundness.

Huge
stand the spindles
into the unland, the trees: there is,
from below, a
light knotted into the air-
mat on which you set the table, for the empty
chairs and their
sabbath splendor, for—

their glory.

Le Menhir

Wachsendes
Steingrau.

Graugestalt, augen-
loser du, Steinblick, mit dem uns
die Erde hervortrat, menschlich,
auf Dunkel-, auf Weissheidewegen,
abends, vor
dir, Himmelsschlucht.

Verkebstes, hierhergekarrt, sank
über den Herzrücken weg. Meer-
mühle mahlte.

Hellflüglig hingst du, früh,
zwischen Ginster und Stein,
kleine Phaläne.

Schwarz, phylakterien-
farben, so wart ihr,
ihr mit-
betenden Schoten.

Le Menhir

Growing
stone-gray.

Gray-shape, more eye-
less you, stone-gaze, with which the
earth emerged for us, human
on dark-, on white-heath-paths,
at dusk, before
you, sky-ravine.

The Concubined, carted here, sank
away over the heart's back. Sea-
mill milled.

Bright-winged you hung, early,
between furze and stone,
little phalaena.

Black, phylactery-
hued, you were all this,
you husks pray-
ing along.

Hinausgekrönt,
hinausgespien in die Nacht.

Bei welchen
Sternen! Lauter
graugeschlagenes Herzhammersilber. Und
Berenikes Haupthaar, auch hier, —ich flocht,
ich zerflocht,
ich flechte, zerflechte.
Ich flechte.

Blauschlucht, in dich
treib ich das Gold. Auch mit ihm, dem
bei Huren und Dirnen vertanen,
komm ich und komm ich. Zu dir,
Geliebte.

Auch mit Fluch und Gebet. Auch mit jeder
der über mich hin-
schwirrenden Keulen: auch sie in eins
geschmolzen, auch sie
phallisch gebündelt zu dir,
Garbe-und-Wort.

Mit Namen, getränkt
von jedem Exil.
Mit Namen und Samen,
mit Namen, getaucht
in alle
Kelche, die vollstehn mit deinem

Crowned out,
spewed out into night.

At what
stars! All
gray-beaten heart-hammer-silver. And
Berenice's Hair, here too—I braided,
I braided to bits,
I braid, braid to bits.
I braid.

Blue-ravine, into you
I drive the gold. With him too, the man
used up by whores and harlots,
I come and I come. To you,
beloved.

With curses and prayers as well. And with each
of the bludgeons
that whiz over me: they, too, smelted
into one, they too
a phallic fascicle,
sheaf-and-word.

With names, steeped
in every exile.
With names and semen,
with names, dipped
in all
chalices that are filled with your

Königsblut, Mensch,—in alle
Kelche der grossen
Ghetto-Rose, aus der
du uns ansiehst, unsterblich von soviel
auf Morgenwegen gestorbenen Toden.

(Und wir sangen die Warschowjanka.
Mit verschilften Lippen, Petrarca.
In Tundra-Ohren, Petrarca.)

Und es steigt eine Erde herauf, die unsre,
diese.
Und wir schicken
keinen der Unsern hinunter
zu dir,
Babel.

royal blood, man—in all
calyces of the great
Ghetto-rose, from which
you watch us, immortal from so many
deaths died on morning-roads.

(And we sang the Varshovyanka.
With sedge-choked lips, Petrarch.
In tundra-ears, Petrarch.)

And there rises an earth, ours,
this one.
And we send
none of us down
to you,
Babel.

Und mit dem Buch aus Tarussa

Все поэты жиды.

—Marina Zwetajewa

Vom
Sternbild des Hundes, vom
Hellstern darin und der Zwerg-
leuchte, die mitwebt
an erdwärts gespiegelten Wegen,

von
Pilgerstäben, auch dort, von Südlichem, fremd
und nachtfasernah
wie unbestattete Worte,
streunend
im Bannkreis erreichter
Ziele und Stelen und Wiegen.

Von
Wahr- und Voraus- und Vorüber-zu-dir-,
von
Hinaufgesagtem,
das dort bereitliegt, einem
der eigenen Herzsteine gleich, die man ausspie
mitsamt ihrem un-
verwüstlichen Uhrwerk, hinaus
in Unland und Unzeit. Von solchem
Ticken und Ticken inmitten
der Kies-Kuben mit
der auf Hyänenspur rückwärts,
aufwärts verfolgbaren
Ahnen-
reihe Derer-

And with the Book from Tarussa

> All poets are Jews.
>
> —Marina Tsvetayeva

Of the
constellation of Canis, of the
bright-star within and the dwarf-
light that also weaves
on roads mirrored earthwards,

of
pilgrim-staffs, there too, of the south, alien
and nightfiber-near
like unsepulchered words,
roaming
in the orbit of attained
goals and stelae and cradles.

Of things
sooth-said and fore-told and spoken over to you,
of things
talked upwards,
on the alert, akin to one
of one's own heart-stones that one spewed out
together with their in-
destructible clockwork, out
into unland and untime. Of such
ticking and ticking amid
the gravel-cubes with
(going back on a hyena spoor
traceable upwards)
the ancestral
line of Those-

vom-Namen-und-Seiner-
Rundschlucht.

Von
einem Baum, von einem.
Ja, auch von ihm. Und vom Wald um ihn her. Vom Wald
Unbetreten, vom
Gedanken, dem er entwuchs, als Laut
und Halblaut und Ablaut und Auslaut, skythisch
zusammengereimt
im Takt
der Verschlagenen-Schläfe,
mit
geatmeten Steppen-
halmen geschrieben ins Herz
der Stundenzäsur—in das Reich,
in der Reiche
weitestes, in
den Grossbinnenreim
jenseits
der Stummvölker-Zone, in dich
Sprachwaage, Wortwaage, Heimat-
waage Exil.

Von diesem Baum, diesem Wald.

Von der Brücken-
quader, von der
er ins Leben hinüber-
prallte, flügge
von Wunden,—vom
Pont Mirabeau.
Wo die Oka nicht mitfliesst. Et quels
amours! (Kyrillisches, Freunde, auch das
ritt ich über die Seine,
ritts übern Rhein.)

of-the-Name-and-Its-
Round-Abyss.

Of
a tree, of one.
Yes, of it too. And of the woods around it. Of the woods
Untrodden, of the
thought they grew from, as sound
and half-sound and changed sound and terminal sound, Scythian
rhymes
in the meter
of the temple of the driven,
with
breathed steppe-
grass written into the heart
of the hour-caesura—into the realm,
the widest of
realms, into
the great internal rhyme
beyond
the zone of mute nations, into yourself
language-scale, word-scale, home-
scale of exile.

Of this tree, these woods.

Of the bridge's
broadstone, from which
he bounced across into
life, full-fledged
by wounds—of the
Pont Mirabeau.
Where the Oka doesn't flow. Et quels
amours! (Cyrillic, friends, I rode
this too across the Seine,
rode it across the Rhine.)

Von einem Brief, von ihm.
Vom Ein-Brief, vom Ost-Brief. Vom harten,
winzigen Worthaufen, vom
unbewaffneten Auge, das er
den drei
Gürtelsternen Orions—Jakobs-
stab, du,
abermals kommst du gegangen!—
zuführt auf der
Himmelskarte, die sich ihm aufschlug.

Vom Tisch, wo das geschah.

Von einem Wort, aus dem Haufen,
an dem er, der Tisch,
zur Ruderbank wurde, vom Oka-Fluss her
und den Wassern.

Vom Nebenwort, das
ein Ruderknecht nachknirscht, ins Spätsommerohr
seiner hell-
hörigen Dolle:

Kolchis.

Of a letter, of it.
Of the one-letter, East-letter. Of the hard and
tiny word-heap, of the
unarmed eye that it
transmits to
the three
belt-stars of Orion—Jacob's
staff, you,
once again you come walking!—
on the
celestial chart that opened for it.

Of the table where this happened.

Of a word, from the heap
on which it, the table
became a galley-seat, from the Oka River
and its waters.

Of the passing word that
a galley-slave gnash-echos, into the late-summer reeds
of his keen-
eared thole-pin:

Colchis.

aus
Atemwende

from
Breath-Turning

Du darfst mich getrost
mit Schnee bewirten:
sooft ich Schulter an Schulter
mit dem Maulbeerbaum schritt durch den Sommer,
schrie sein jüngstes
Blatt.

By all means
regale me with snow:
whenever I strode through the summer
shoulder to shoulder with the mulberry tree,
its youngest leaf
shrieked.

In den Flüssen nördlich der Zukunft
werf ich das Netz aus, das du
zögernd beschwerst
mit von Steinen geschriebenen
Schatten.

In the rivers north of the future
I cast out the net that you,
wavering, weigh down
with shadows written by
stones.

Die Zahlen, im Bund
mit der Bilder Verhängnis
und Gegen-
verhängnis.

Der drübergestülpte
Schädel, an dessen
schlafloser Schläfe ein irr-
lichternder Hammer
all das im Welttakt
besingt.

The numerals, in league
with the doom
and anti-
doom
of the images.

The skull that covers them,
and on whose
sleepless temple a will-
o'-the-wisp hammer
carols all this in
world-rhythm.

Stehen, im Schatten
des Wundenmals in der Luft.

Für-niemand-und-nichts-Stehn.
Unerkannt,
für dich
allein.

Mit allem, was darin Raum hat,
auch ohne
Sprache.

Standing, in the shadow
of the cicatrise in the air.

Standing for no-one and nothing.
Unrecognized,
for you
alone.

With all that has space within,
even without
language.

Fadensonnen
über der grauschwarzen Ödnis.
Ein baum-
hoher Gedanke
greift sich den Lichtton: es sind
noch Lieder zu singen jenseits
der Menschen.

Thread-suns
over the gray-black wasteland.
A tree-
high thought
strikes the note of light: there are
still songs to sing beyond
mankind.

Wortaufschüttung, vulkanisch,
meerüberrauscht.

Oben
der flutende Mob
der Gegengeschöpfe: er
flaggte—Abbild und Nachbild
kreuzen eitel zeithin.

Bis du den Wortmond hinaus-
schleuderst, von dem her
das Wunder Ebbe geschieht
und der herz-
förmige Krater
nackt für die Anfänge zeugt,
die Königs-
geburten.

Word-embankment, volcanic,
overroared by ocean.

Above,
the tidal mob
of anti-creatures: it
signaled—image and after-image
cruise vainly timewards.

Until you hurl out the word—
moon from which
the miracle of ebb occurs
and the heart-
shaped crater
testifies naked for the beginnings,
the births
of kings.

Weggebeizt vom
Strahlenwind deiner Sprache
das bunte Gerede des An-
erlebten—das hundert-
züngige Mein-
gedicht, das Genicht.

Aus-
gewirbelt,
frei
der Weg durch den menschen-
gestaltigen Schnee,
den Büsserschnee, zu
den gastlichen
Gletscherstuben und -tischen.

Tief
in der Zeitenschrunde,
beim
Wabeneis
wartet, ein Atemkristall,
dein unumstössliches
Zeugnis.

Cauterized by the
radiant wind of your language
the palaver of in-stilled
ex–perience—the hundred-
tongued perjury-
poem, the no-em.

Whirled
out,
free,
the road through the human-
shaped snow,
the penitent-snow, to
the cordial
glacier-rooms and -tables.

Deep
in the time-crevasse,
by the
honeycomb-ice,
there waits, as a breath-crystal,
your unimpeachable
testimony.

Vom grossen
Augen-
losen
aus deinen Augen geschöpft:

der sechs-
kantige, absageweisse
Findling.

Eine Blindenhand, sternhart auch sie
vom Namen-Durchwandern,
ruht auf ihm, so
lang wie auf dir,
Esther.

Drained by the great
Eye-
less one
from your eyes:

the six-
edged refusal-white
foundling.

A blindman's hand, star-hard too
from roaming through names,
rests on him as
long as on you,
Esther.

Singbarer Rest—der Umriss
dessen, der durch
die Sichelschrift lautlos hindurchbrach,
abseits, am Schneeort.

Quirlend
unter Kometen-
brauen
die Blickmasse, auf
die der verfinsterte winzige
Herztrabant zutreibt
mit dem
draussen erjagten Funken.

—Entmündigte Lippe, melde,
dass etwas geschieht, noch immer,
unweit von dir.

Singable remainder—the outline
of him who mutely
broke through the sickle-script,
aside, at the snow-place.

Whirling
under comet-
brows,
the gaze-mass towards
which the darkened, diminutive
heart-satellite drifts
with the
spark ensnared outside.

—Interdicted lip, report
that something is happening still,
not far from you.

Am weissen Gebetriemen—der
Herr dieser Stunde
war
ein Wintergeschöpf, ihm
zulieb
geschah, was geschah—
biss sich mein kletternder Mund fest, noch einmal,
als er dich suchte, Rauchspur
du, droben,
in Frauengestalt,
du auf der Reise zu meinen
Feuergedanken im Schwarzkies
jenseits der Spaltworte, durch
die ich dich gehn sah, hoch-
beinig und
den schwerlippigen eignen
Kopf
auf dem von meinen
tödlich genauen
Händen
lebendigen Körper.

Sag deinen dich
bis in die Schluchten hinein-
begleitenden Fingern, wie
ich dich kannte, wie weit
ich dich ins Tiefe stiess, wo
dich mein bitterster Traum
herzher beschlief, im Bett
meines unablösbaren Namens.

On the white prayer-thong (the
lord of this hour
was
a winter creature, what
happened happened
for its sake)
my climbing teeth bit in, once again
when they sought you, smoke-wisp
you, aloft,
in female-shape,
you on the way to my
fire-thoughts in the black gravel
beyond the rift-words, through
which I saw you walk, high-
limbed and
your heavy-lipped own
head
on the body living
by my
deadly accurate
hands.

Tell your fingers,
accompanying you into
the very ravines, how
I knew you, how far
I thrust you into the depth where
my bitterest dream lay with
you, heart-hence, in the bed
of my irredeemable name.

Landschaft mit Urnenwesen.
Gespräche
von Rauchmund zu Rauchmund.

Sie essen:
die Tollhäusler-Trüffel, ein Stück
unvergrabner Poesie,
fand Zunge und Zahn.

Eine Träne rollt in ihr Auge zurück.

Die linke, verwaiste
Hälfte der Pilger-
muschel—sie schenkten sie dir,
dann banden sie dich—
leuchtet lauschend den Raum aus:

das Klinkerspiel gegen den Tod
kann beginnen.

Landscape with urn-beings.
Conversations
from smoke-mouth to smoke-mouth

They eat:
the bedlamite-truffle, a piece
of unburied poetry,
found tongue and tooth.

A tear rolls back into its eye.

The orphaned left
half of the pilgrim's
shell (they gave it to you,
then they tied you up),
listening, lights out the space:

the clinker-playing against death
can begin.

Die Gauklertrommel,
von meinem Herzgroschen laut.

Die Sprossen der Leiter, über
die Odysseus, mein Affe, nach Ithaka klettert,
rue de Longchamp, eine Stunde
nach dem verschütteten Wein:

tu das zum Bild,
das uns heimwürfelt in
den Becher, in dem ich bei dir lieg,
unausspielbar.

The juggler's drum,
loud from my heart-penny.

The rungs of the ladder up
which Odysseus, my monkey, climbs to Ithaca,
on Rue de Longchamp, one hour
after the spilled wine:

add this to the image
that gambles us home to
the dicecup in which I lie with you,
never to be played out.

In Prag

Der halbe Tod,
grossgesäugt mit unserm Leben,
lag aschenbildwahr um uns her—

auch wir
tranken noch immer, seelenverkreuzt, zwei Degen,
an Himmelssteine genäht, wortblutgeboren
im Nachtbett,

grösser und grösser
wuchsen wir durcheinander, es gab
keinen Namen mehr für
das, was uns trieb (einer der Wieviel-
unddreissig
war mein lebendiger Schatten,
der die Wahnstiege hochklomm zu dir?),

ein Turm,
baute der Halbe sich ins Wohin,
ein Hradschin
aus lauter Goldmacher-Nein,

Knochen-Hebräisch,
zu Sperma zermahlen,
rann durch die Sanduhr,
die wir durchschwammen, zwei Träume jetzt, läutend
wider die Zeit, auf den Plätzen.

In Prague

Half of death,
suckled along with our life,
lay about us as true as an ash-image—

we too
still drank, soul-crossed, two swords,
sewn to sky-stones, born in word-blood
in the night-bed,

bigger and bigger
we grew in (con-) fusion, there was
no name anymore for
what drove us (one of the thirty-
what?
was my living shadow,
that climbed the chimerical stairway up to you),

a tower,
the half built itself into the where,
a Hradčany
all of alchemist-no,

bone-Hebrew,
ground into sperm,
ran through the sand-glass,
in which we swam, two dreams now, tolling
against time, on the squares.

Aschenglorie hinter
deinen erschüttert-verknoteten
Händen am Dreiweg.

Pontisches Einstmals: hier,
ein Tropfen,
auf
dem ertrunkenen Ruderblatt,
tief
im versteinerten Schwur,
rauscht es auf.

(Auf dem senkrechten
Atemseil, damals,
höher als oben,
zwischen zwei Schmerzknoten, während
der blanke
Tatarenmond zu uns heraufklomm,
grub ich mich in dich und in dich.)

Aschen-
glorie hinter
euch Dreiweg-
Händen.

Das vor euch, vom Osten her, Hin-
gewürfelte, furchtbar.

Niemand
zeugt für den
Zeugen.

Ash-glory behind
your shaken-knotted
hands on the three-forked road.

Pontic once-upon: here,
a drop
on
the drowned oar-blade,
deep
in the petrified vow,
it roars up.

(On the perpendicular
breath-rope, at that time,
higher than above,
between two pain-knots, while
the shiny
Tartar moon climbed up to us,
I burrowed into you and into you.)

Ash-
glory behind
your three-forked
hands.

The thing diced before you
from the East, dreadful.

No one
bears witness for the
witness.

Cello-Einsatz
von hinter dem Schmerz:

die Gewalten, nach Gegen-
himmeln gestaffelt,
wälzen Undeutbares vor
Einflugschneise und Einfahrt,

der
erklommene Abend
steht voller Lungengeäst,

zwei
Brandwolken Atem
graben im Buch,
das der Schläfenlärm aufschlug,

etwas wird wahr,

zwölfmal erglüht
das von Pfeilen getroffene Drüben,

die Schwarz-
blütige trinkt
des Schwarzblütigen Samen,

alles ist weniger, als
es ist,
alles ist mehr.

Cello entry
from behind the hurt:

the powers, in echelons
toward anti-skies,
roll the inexplicable in front of
flying-lane and entrance,

the
climbed evening
is filled with lung-branchings,

two
fire-clouds of breath
dig in the book
that the temple-noise opened,

something turns true,

the yonder pierced by arrows
glows twelve times,

the black-
blossomed female drinks
the seed of the black-blossomed male,

all is less than
it is,
all is more.

Frihed

Im Haus zum gedoppelten Wahn,
wo die Steinboote fliegen
überm
Weisskönigs-Pier, den Geheimnissen zu,
wo das endlich
abgenabelte
Orlog-Wort kreuzt,

bin ich, von Schilfmark Genährte,
in dir, auf
Wildenten-Teichen,

ich singe—

was sing ich?

Der Mantel
des Saboteurs
mit den roten, den weissen
Kreisen um die
Einschuss-
stellen
—durch sie
erblickst du das mit uns fahrende
frei-
sternige Oben—
deckt uns jetzt zu,

der Grünspan-Adel vom Kai,
mit seinen Backstein-Gedanken

Frihed *

In the house of the double delusion,
where the stone-boats fly
over the
white-king's pier, towards the mysteries,
where the war-word,
its navelstring cut at last,
cruises,

I, nourished on reed-marrow,
am in you, on
wildduck-ponds,

I sing—

what do I sing?

The saboteur's
cloak
with the red, the white
circles around the
bullet-
holes
(through them
you glimpse the
free-
starred Above that travels with us)
covers us up now,

the verdigris-aristocracy of the wharf,
with its brick-thoughts

rund um die Stirn,
häuft den Geist rings, den Gischt,

schnell
verblühn die Geräusche
diesseits und jenseits der Trauer,

die näher-
segelnde
Eiterzacke der Krone
in eines Schief-
geborenen Aug
dichtet
dänisch.

around its forehead,
piles the spirit in a circle, the spray,

quickly
the noises wither
on either side of grief,

the close-
hugging
pus-point of the crown
in the eye
of a Skew-born
indites
Danish.

Schlickende, dann
krautige Stille der Ufer.

Die eine Schleuse noch. Am
Warzenturm, mit
Brackigem übergossen,
mündest du ein.

Vor dir, in
den rudernden Riesensporangien,
sichelt, als keuchten dort Worte,
ein Glanz.

Mud-choking, then
herbaceous hush of the banks.

The one last sluice. At the
wart-tower, steeped
in brackishness,
you disembogue.

Before you, in
the gigantic, rowing sporangiums,
a brightness reaps
as though words were gasping.

Der mit Himmeln geheizte
Feuerriss durch die Welt.

Die Wer da?-Rufe
in seinem Innern:

durch dich hier hindurch
auf den Schild
der Ewigen Wanze gespiegelt,
umschnüffelt von Falsch und Verstört,

die unendliche Schleife ziehend, trotzdem,
die schiffbar bleibt für die un-
getreidelte Antwort.

The sky-fueled
fire-rip through the world.

The Who-goes-there?-calls
inside it:

mirrored through you here
on the shield-shell
of the Eternal Bedbug,
sniffed at by False and Bewildered,

drawing, nonetheless, the endless loop,
that remains navigable for the un-
hauled answer.

Einmal,
da hörte ich ihn,
da wusch er die Welt,
ungesehn, nachtlang,
wirklich.

Eins und Unendlich,
vernichtet,
ichten.

Licht war. Rettung.

Once
I heard him,
he was washing the world,
unseen, nightlong,
real.

One and Infinity,
dieing,
were I'ing.

Light was. Salvation.

Notes on the Poems

Train-Tracks, Roadsides, Vacant Lots, Rubble

The *Augarten* is a huge park in Vienna. The Marchfeld, a long plain in eastern Austria, was the scene of many historic military encounters.

The Sluice

Kaddish is the Jewish prayer spoken at a funeral, *Yiskor* the memorial prayer for the dead.

Dioecious, Eternal One, art thou

Dioecious, from a Greek word meaning literally "two-housed," refers to plants and animals that have separate male and female organs. The German word *zweihäusig*, literally "two-housed," conveys the biological idea and, like the Greek, the notion of a double dwelling, from which the ambisexual metaphoric content of the poem is developed.

Benedicta

Gebentsht is the past participle of the Yiddish verb *bentschen*, to bless, to speak the Jewish prayer that ends a meal. It is cognate with the German word *gebenedeiet*, "blessed, blest," and both words derive from the Latin *benedicta*.

Havdalah

Havdalah, derived from a Hebrew word that means a "separation," is the Jewish ceremony ending the Sabbath on Saturday afternoon.

Frihed

Frihed is Danish for "freedom."

About the Author

PAUL CELAN was born in 1920, the son of Austrian Jews in Czernovitz, Bukovina, a multilingual area that had become part of Romania after the breakup of the Hapsburg Empire. Following the Stalin-Hitler Pact, Bukovina was occupied by the Soviet and then by the Nazi army. Celan's parents were murdered in a death camp, but he managed to survive the war in a forced-labor camp. In 1947, he spent some time in Vienna and then settled in Paris, becoming a teacher of German at the École Normale. During the next twenty years he published seven volumes of poems in Germany, garnering a number of important awards. He also translated numerous foreign poets, including Mandelshtamm, Ungaretti, Du Bouchet, and Shakespeare. He died in Paris in April, 1970.

About the Translator

JOACHIM NEUGROSCHEL grew up in New York, taking his B.A. in Comparative Literature at Columbia University. His poetry has appeared in various underground journals, and he is co-editor of *Extensions*, a magazine of experimental writing. In addition, he has translated many foreign authors, including Racine, Moliere, Chekhov, Arp, Dali. He is a staff reviewer on *Arts Magazine*, and, at the moment, he is preparing an American edition of writings by the French artist Jean Dubuffet for publication next year.